W9-ALJ-410

VOTE!

WOMEN'S FIGHT FOR ACCESS TO THE BALLOT BOX

CORAL CELESTE FRAZER

TWENTY-FIRST CENTURY BOOKS / MINNEAPOLIS

To Muz, with love

Acknowledgments

Once again, I am indebted to Peg Goldstein for outstanding editing. She has worked her usual magic and made the text immeasurably clearer and more precise. My gratitude also to Domenica Di Piazza for ensuring that every word and image was up to a rigorous standard. The TFCB team always makes their books look outstanding. Thank you to Laura Westlund for the infographics and Giliane Mansfeldt for securing the photos and other images.

Victoria Chamberlin, Natasha Hutcheson, Helen Lindsay, and Margaret Meyer provided feedback on early chapters. Thanks for your insights and support. I love talking writing with you ladies.

Thanks are not enough for Michael Frazer, who read the whole manuscript and also provided meals, cups of tea, and endless repetitions of "You can do it. I have faith in you" as deadlines pressed near. Oren Frazer put up with countless suffrage anecdotes without complaining—too much. Sometimes he even found them interesting. I love you both without bounds.

Twenty-First Century Books
An imprint of Lerner Publishing Group, Inc.
241 First Avenue North
Minneapolis, MN 55401 USA

For reading levels and more information, look up this title at www.lernerbooks.com.

Library of Congress Cataloging-in-Publication Data

Names: Frazer, Coral Celeste, author.
Title: Vote! : women's fight for access to the ballot box / Coral Celeste Frazer.
Description: Minneapolis, Minnesota : Twenty-First Century Books, [2019] | Includes
    bibliographical references and index. |
Identifiers: LCCN 2018038960 (print) | LCCN 2018040907 (ebook) |
    ISBN 9781541562653 (eb pdf) | ISBN 9781541528154 (library binding : alk. paper)
Subjects: LCSH: Women—Suffrage—United States—History—Juvenile literature.
Classification: LCC JK1898 (ebook) | LCC JK1898 .F73 2019 (print) | DDC
    324.6/230973—dc23

LC record available at https://lccn.loc.gov/2018038960

Manufactured in the United States of America
1-44694-35530-1/24/2019

CONTENTS

1

"STAY AT HOME"

On a sunny spring day in March 1913, more than five thousand women lined up to march down Pennsylvania Avenue, a famed street in Washington, DC, that connects the White House and the US Capitol. Dressed in matching capes and caps, color-coded by profession or by state, the women were ready to show the nation that they wanted the right to vote. Some rode in cars while most walked. Their ranks included nine marching bands, three trumpeters, two thousand yellow banners, twenty-four historically themed floats, six golden chariots, and four groups on horseback.

As the parade set off, one hundred dancers in filmy white dresses began a ballet on the marble steps of the Treasury Building, where the parade would end. The climax of their performance was set to coincide with the arrival of the first marchers. So forty-five minutes after the parade began, women in costumes representing the qualities of liberty, justice, charity, hope, and peace swept down the marble steps and joined a woman dressed as Columbia—a goddesslike figure representing the United States. Together, the performers waited to greet the marchers.

But the marchers did not arrive as expected. Though their waiting supporters did not know it, they were fighting their way through masses of unruly spectators, who had slipped past police barriers to block their route.

Costumed dancers, including a performer dressed as Columbia (a symbol of the United States), present a dance in front of the US Treasury Building. The dancers participated in this 1913 parade in the nation's capital to promote women's suffrage.

Every step forward was a battle. Even when women in the parade drove cars slowly to part the crowd, loud, aggressive, male protesters poured in to fill the gaps. Many of the men were drunk. They hurled abuse at the marching women. "Women were spit upon, slapped in the face, tripped up, pelted with burning cigar stubs, and insulted by jeers and obscene language too vile to print or repeat," according to an account in the newspaper *Woman's Journal.* Even worse, the police did nothing to control the mob. To the marchers' fury, police officers stood by and laughed. One told the women, "There would be nothing like this if you would stay at home."

The police officer's wish that women would just "stay at home" reflected the attitude of large numbers of American men of the era. By 1913 American women had been fighting for the right to vote for more than sixty-five years. And for longer than that, women had heard men say that they should just stay home—that they should not be involved in politics, that they should not vote or run for political office or work outside the home or make claims to equality with men.

But change was afoot. "Washington has been disgraced," proclaimed the *Woman's Journal* after the attack on the marchers. Many other Americans—including many men—agreed. The attack horrified the public, won sympathy for the marchers, and convinced many that it was time for women to have equal access to the ballot box.

"THE HUSBAND AND THE WIFE ARE ONE"

When the United States was a young country, in the early nineteenth century, its female citizens—especially married women—had few legal rights. When an American woman married, the law no longer considered her a separate person. In the United States, laws that controlled women's lives were based on the writings of British legal scholar William Blackstone. He said, "The husband and the wife are one, and that one is the husband." So a woman's rights, property, and legal responsibilities went to her husband as soon as she married. Literally, everything she owned, including land, money, and even her own clothes and possessions, belonged to her husband. If she worked outside the home, her wages belonged to her husband as well.

In this era, American women could not enter into contracts, sue or be sued, serve on juries, or vote. Mothers had no legal custody of their children. The father had sole responsibility for making decisions about their welfare. He could apprentice them to a master to learn a trade or appoint someone other than the mother to be the children's guardian if he died. Women were not allowed to divorce their husbands, except in the most abusive situations. If a couple did divorce, the husband always kept the children. Married women did not even have the right to control their own bodies. They could not legally refuse to have sex with their husbands, and in this era before effective and legal contraception, they had no ability to control when they became pregnant.

Nineteenth-century children were typically taught at home, by parents or tutors, or in small local schools. Boys and girls went to primary school at roughly the same rates. But higher education was exclusively for men. No American colleges or universities admitted women until Oberlin College in Ohio became the first to do so in 1837.

Female seminaries were as close as a young woman could get to a college education. These schools, started by women, taught many of the same subjects as colleges and universities, including composition, algebra, history, natural philosophy (science), French, and sometimes Latin. Some schools also offered training in needlework, art, and music. But parents and doctors also feared that too much intellectual effort would strain young women's brains or even harm their chances of bearing children.

Seminaries also placed a strong focus on the "cult of true womanhood"—the idea that women should be domestic, modest, maternal, religious, cultured, idle, and subservient to men. This meant they should take care of their homes, husbands, and children, and leave things like employment, politics, and public speaking to men.

Many American women did work outside the home. These were poor women and girls who labored in factories, sometimes for twelve to sixteen hours a day. Though they worked just as hard, female laborers were paid far less than male laborers.

A TIME FOR REFORM

In the early United States, each state determined voter qualifications for local, state, and national elections. Most states allowed only white men to vote and only if they owned land of a certain size or value. New Jersey was one state that for a short time (1776 to 1807) allowed women to vote, but only if they met the state's property requirements. And since married women could not own property, they could not vote, even in New Jersey.

By 1800 most states had reduced or dropped their property requirements for voting. About 80 percent of white American males could vote. However, women, free and enslaved African Americans, American Indians, many immigrants, and some poor white men remained disenfranchised (without voting rights). This meant that most Americans had no say in the laws that controlled their lives.

Like other American institutions, most churches taught that women were inferior to men and had a duty to obey them. But churches were also one of the few acceptable public places for women to meet and organize. In church groups, women could gather to socialize, to help others, and to help one another. For example, some women's church groups raised money to support orphans.

Small, local efforts such as these sometimes grew into larger efforts to improve society as a whole. And much in the United States cried out for improvement. Living

Child and adult slaves, photographed around 1860, stand in a cotton field on a plantation near Savannah, Georgia. They have gathered large basketsful of cotton fiber, which will be processed and woven into cloth. Many Americans who joined the abolition movement—the fight to end slavery—also fought for women's suffrage.

conditions for the poor were wretched. Prisons were inhumane. Alcoholism was rampant. Slavery was the most urgent and divisive issue of the mid-nineteenth century. Almost four million African American people were enslaved. Enslaved women and men had no rights whatsoever. They belonged to white masters who forced them to work for no pay. Their overseers and masters could whip or rape them with no consequences. Slave owners frequently sold slaves to new masters, ripping families apart.

American abolitionists looked on slavery with horror and worked toward ending it. But many Americans supported slavery. They believed that black people were inferior to white people. They felt that white owners should control the lives of black slaves. Some even claimed that slavery was beneficial to black people because it exposed them to the values of white, Christian society. The economy of the American South was based on slavery, so support for slavery was high in southern states. And many people in the North supported slavery.

Two women who bravely threw themselves into the fight to end slavery were Sarah Grimké and Angelina Grimké Weld. The Grimké sisters were from a rich South Carolina family. Their father, the chief justice of the Supreme Court of South Carolina, owned a large plantation and hundreds of slaves. The sisters became convinced that slavery was wrong. After their father died in 1819, Sarah Grimké (who was twelve years older than her sister was) and then Angelina Grimké left home and moved to Philadelphia, Pennsylvania. There they joined a community of Quakers, a religious group that opposed slavery. Quakers also believed that women and men were equal. The group allowed women to become ministers, which was unheard of in most other American churches and religious communities at the time.

In 1836 Sarah Grimké wrote *Epistle to the Clergy of the Southern States.* In this pamphlet, she argued that slavery was un-Christian. That year Angelina Grimké wrote *An Appeal to the Christian Women of the South.* This pamphlet urged southern women to fight against slavery by first reading and praying on the subject, and then speaking and acting on it. These writings angered many slave owners. Some South Carolinians burned copies of Angelina's pamphlet. Others threatened the sisters' lives.

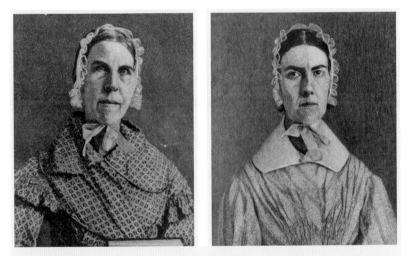

One of the first calls for women's rights in the United States came from Sarah Grimké (*left*). She and her sister Angelina Grimké Weld (*right*) also spoke about the evils of slavery.

A UNIQUE MOMENT IN HISTORY

Throughout history, in most times and places, women have had fewer rights than men. The degree of inequality has varied by time and place. In ancient Egypt (3100–332 BCE), among the upper classes, differences in the legal rights of women and men were relatively small. Well-off ancient Egyptian women had the right to inherit property, participate in legal contracts, sue or be sued, and adopt children.

In ancient India, from 1500 to 500 BCE, women had some rights. Girls and boys had equal access to education. Women wrote poetry, produced art, and participated in religious and philosophical debates alongside men. Unmarried women had some property rights, although once they were married, these rights disappeared.

In Sparta, a Greek city-state that flourished from the seventh to the fourth centuries BCE, women could be educated, own property, participate in athletics, and interact with men in the public sphere. But the Spartans were unusual among the ancient Greeks. Most other city-states restricted women's rights. Women's status was particularly low in ancient Athens, the Greek city-state that established the world's first democracy. Athenian women could not participate in this democracy because they were not citizens. Athenian women were uneducated and mostly confined to their homes. Girls were the property of their fathers until they married. Then they became the property of their husbands.

For thousands of years, women remained subservient to men. But in the eighteenth century, ideas about equality and human rights began to change. In parts of Europe and North America, citizens overthrew monarchies (rule by kings and queens) and demanded democratically elected governments. With the rise of new democracies, women began to push for equal rights with men. Women's rights movements began in the United States and Canada, in Britain and other parts of Europe, and in Australia and New Zealand. Eventually, the fight for women's equality spread to virtually every corner of the globe.

The sisters stepped up their abolition efforts. They traveled to northeastern states, talking about their views to small groups of women. Many northerners had had no direct contact with slavery and wanted to hear what the sisters had to say. As they spoke to larger audiences of men and women, the Grimkés drew more and more criticism. Speaking in public was unheard of for women of this era. Even their Quaker community disapproved of the Grimkés' outspokenness. All the same, in 1838, Angelina Grimké gave a speech to the Massachusetts state legislature. She was the first American woman to address a legislative body.

"TAKE THEIR FEET FROM OFF OUR NECKS"

As they fought to topple the institution of slavery, the Grimkés and other American women were also aware of the injustices they faced in their own lives. They opposed laws and customs that limited their property rights, education, and wages. These women wanted a voice in government. They wanted lawmakers to listen when they said that slavery was wrong and that women were being treated unfairly.

In *Letters on the Equality of the Sexes and the Condition of Woman*—a series of letters later published as a pamphlet—Sarah Grimké argued against the common belief that the Bible held women to be inferior to men. She asked that women be allowed to take their proper place in society as the equals of men. She demanded educational reform and equal wages for men and women. She wrote, "I ask no favors for my sex. I surrender not our claims to equality. All I ask our brethren is, that they will take their feet from off our necks and permit us to stand upright on that ground which God designed us to occupy."

WHAT IS SUFFRAGE?

The term *suffrage* comes from the Latin word *suffragium*, meaning "a vote" or "the right to vote." In the twenty-first century, Americans generally use the term *women's suffrage*, to refer to women's right to vote. But in the nineteenth century, Americans said *woman suffrage*. People who fought for women to have the right to vote were suffragists. In Britain some of the women who fought for suffrage adopted the nickname suffragettes.

But US lawmakers did not take women's opinions seriously. Why should they? Women could not vote them out of office. To change the laws that oppressed them and others, a small group of women decided they needed suffrage—the right to vote. This was a radical idea. Most Americans—men and women alike—found it outrageous and ridiculous. Voting was clearly a man's job. First, elections were rowdy affairs, sometimes held in the local saloon, not an acceptable place for women. And many Americans thought that women were not fit to take part in politics. Most believed that women were fundamentally different from men. According to this view, men were rational, logical, and practical, while women were emotional, intuitive, and impulsive. Though they could be wise and loving mothers and wives, women were simply incapable of making smart political decisions. Nor was it fair to ask them to take on the burden of politics. Their lives were already full with the tasks of family, home, charity, and church.

What's more, most Americans believed that women did not need the vote. According to this belief, as the head of his household, a man cast a ballot for the entire family. Women could influence their husbands and sons through gentle persuasion, and that was enough. The thinking went that if women had their own vote, it would disrupt the harmony of the family.

These ideas were deeply entrenched in American life and society in the mid-nineteenth century. Convincing the public that women belonged in politics would be a huge task.

2

GENERALS OF THE WOMEN'S MOVEMENT

Elizabeth Cady was born on November 12, 1815, in Johnstown, New York. Her mother, Margaret Livingston Cady, came from a prominent family. Her father, Daniel Cady, was a successful lawyer, politician, and judge. The Cadys lived in a mansion in the center of town, with a dozen servants. The house was always full of children, law students, and other visitors.

Elizabeth was the seventh of eleven children. Large families were common. But in this era before vaccines and effective medical treatments, many children died young from diseases such as typhoid, scarlet fever, cholera, whooping cough, and diphtheria. In the Cady family, four boys and two girls died in childhood. Elizabeth's one remaining brother died at the age of twenty, after a sudden, short illness. The entire family was devastated. Elizabeth was then ten years old. To comfort her grieving father, she went into the family's darkened parlor and climbed onto his lap. They sat in silence for a while. Finally, he heaved a sigh and said, "Oh my daughter, I wish you were a boy!" The little girl threw her arms around his neck and replied, "I will try to be all my brother was." Cady's wish that his daughter was a boy—his wish that he still had a living son—reflected a widespread attitude in the nineteenth century. Society valued males more than females.

Elizabeth was a sociable and fun-loving girl who also enjoyed studying. Until she was fifteen, she attended the Johnstown Academy, a coeducational private school. She enjoyed competing with the boys in the classroom and on the playground, and she was the only girl in some of her advanced mathematics and language classes. After graduation, she wanted to go on to college along with her male classmates, but her father sent her to Troy Female Seminary instead. The classes were far too easy for her, and she resented the strict rules.

As a young girl, Elizabeth had watched women tearfully consult her father for legal advice. She took note of the passages he showed them, which explained why they had no legal rights. She wished she could rip all those laws from the law books, but her father said that laws could not be changed so easily. She wanted to study law, as her father had, but law schools in this era did not accept women. So she spent most of her early twenties attending parties and dances, riding horses, and visiting friends—typical pastimes for wealthy young American women.

Then she fell in love with Henry Stanton, a professional abolitionist. Antislavery societies paid him to travel around the country giving speeches, collecting petitions, holding conventions, and organizing local communities to fight against slavery. Her family disapproved of the match. Her father thought Henry was too radical because of his abolitionist views and not a good financial prospect. After some hesitation, she married him in 1840. Usually, women promised to obey their husbands in their wedding vows, but she refused to include that promise in her vows.

For their honeymoon, Stanton took his wife to London, where he was a delegate from the American and Foreign Anti-Slavery Society to the World Anti-Slavery Convention of 1840. In London, Elizabeth Cady Stanton met Lucretia Mott, who soon became her close friend and mentor. Mott, who was twenty-two years older than Elizabeth Cady Stanton, was a Quaker minister, a devoted wife, a loving mother to six children, and a fervent abolitionist. Like many other Quakers who were committed to abolition, she refused to wear cotton cloth or to eat cane sugar because slaves picked the cotton and cut the cane. She also helped slaves escape to freedom in Canada, which abolished slavery in 1833. Her home was one of the stops on the so-called Underground Railroad. This network of secret routes and safe houses helped slaves escape to freedom. Lucretia Mott was in London as a representative

Elizabeth Cady Stanton poses with two of her sons in 1848. That year Stanton and Lucretia Mott held the Seneca Falls Convention, where Stanton passionately argued for women's suffrage.

of the Philadelphia Female Anti-Slavery Society, which she had helped found.

The presence of Lucretia Mott and seven other female delegates sparked a huge controversy. The convention organizers did not want women to participate. They did not think it was appropriate for women to speak in public. But some of the men from the United States argued strongly in favor of seating the women. The men argued for hours about the issue. Finally, the convention delegates voted, and the women's side lost. The female delegates had to sit and watch from a roped-off section with other guests. They were not allowed to speak.

Though not a delegate herself, Elizabeth Cady Stanton was furious. She was filled with contempt for the men's reasoning and what she considered their cruel treatment of "their own mothers, with the rest of womankind."

The seeds of her future activism had been planted. That evening, walking back to the boardinghouse that served as their home during the convention, Elizabeth Cady Stanton and Lucretia Mott decided to hold a convention of their own. This one would address the rights of women. It took eight years to complete this plan.

THE SENECA FALLS CONVENTION

In 1847 Elizabeth and Henry Stanton were living in Seneca Falls, New York. By then they had three sons, who were often sick, and she spent most of her time cleaning and cooking and caring for them. Henry Stanton had studied law and opened a law practice after their wedding, and he was frequently away from home on business. He was active in local politics and continued to fight for abolition. She envied his freedom. She loved being a mother but resented the tedium of her life. She wanted excitement and intellectual stimulation.

On July 13, 1848, she met with Lucretia Mott and three other friends. The women realized that many of their problems—their boredom and their feelings of isolation and of being smothered by the demands of housework and childcare—came from the way society treated women. They decided to hold a convention to discuss "the social, civil, and religious condition and rights of women."

The women wasted no time finding a venue and contacting the local newspaper. The next day, they ran an announcement in the *Seneca County Courier*, inviting the public to their women's rights convention in the Wesleyan Methodist Chapel on July 19 to 20. The following Sunday, the women met again to plan their agenda. They looked to the US Declaration of Independence for inspiration. Calling their document the Declaration of Rights and Sentiments, they started with the idea that "all men and women are created equal." (The Declaration of Independence states that all men are created equal.) They made a list of resolutions, which participants would vote on at the convention:

- Wives should have equal rights with husbands.
- Women should have the right to own property.
- Mothers should have guardianship over their children.
- Women should have equal access to education and the right to be doctors, lawyers, and ministers. (Only Quakers allowed women ministers at this time.)
- Married working women should keep their own pay.
- Women should be paid as much as men doing the same job.

The women agreed, and their husbands were sympathetic. But Elizabeth Cady Stanton proposed one final resolution: women should fight for the right to vote. Lucretia Mott thought demanding the vote would make the women look ridiculous. Henry Stanton agreed. Nevertheless, Elizabeth Cady Stanton was firm. The right to vote was essential. It would bring the power to win all other reforms for women, so she included it in the list of resolutions.

Turnout at the convention was greater than they had dared to expect. More than one hundred men and women showed up on the first day. Even more came the next. James Mott, Lucretia's husband, presided over the meeting. To have a woman chair a convention was unthinkable, even for these radical women. But Elizabeth Cady Stanton did speak at the meeting—it was her first public speech. She read the Declaration of Rights and Sentiments aloud. And before the debate and vote on the resolutions, she argued passionately for woman suffrage.

The suffrage resolution would likely have failed without the support of Frederick Douglass. Douglass was a former slave and a charismatic and influential speaker. He lectured for the American Anti-Slavery Society and published a widely respected newspaper called the *North Star*. Douglass echoed Elizabeth Cady Stanton's views, arguing that "the power to choose rulers and make laws was the right by which all [other rights] could be secured." With Douglass's support, the suffrage resolution passed but just barely.

After the convention, newspapers across the Northeast mocked and scolded the women for their demands. The criticism didn't faze Elizabeth Cady Stanton. She was delighted that major papers were discussing their ideas. "It will start women thinking, and men too, and when men and women think about a new question, the first step in progress is taken."

The Seneca Falls Convention set off a wave of similar meetings and conferences. Tied to home by her young children, Stanton could not travel as she would have liked to. So she wrote newspaper articles and sent letters to be read at conventions she could not attend. She studied, read, and reflected on women's rights. Meanwhile, she had two more sons and two daughters—seven children in all. She longed to devote more time and energy to improving the lives of women and winning the all-important right to vote. But that would have to wait until her children were older.

"I MUST SPEAK FOR THE WOMEN"

Lucy Stone was born three years after Elizabeth Cady Stanton, on August 13, 1818. The Stones had a farm outside Brookfield, Massachusetts. Lucy's mother put her five young children to bed and milked eight cows the night before she gave birth to

Lucy. After learning that she had given birth to a girl, Hannah Stone said, "Oh dear! I am sorry it's a girl. A woman's lot is so hard."

Life was not easy for Hannah Stone, who worked long days cooking, cleaning, canning, churning butter, milking cows, tending the garden, weaving fabric, knitting socks, taking care of her children, and sewing shoes at home for a local shoe manufacturer. As soon as they were old enough, Lucy and her sisters helped with the chores—including sewing shoes.

Lucy's father was a hardworking man with a temper and a tendency to drink too much. Despite his lack of support, Lucy was determined to go to college. For nine years, during her teens and early twenties, she alternated between teaching in local schools to earn money and going to school to prepare for college entrance exams. She also read abolitionist literature and the Grimké sisters' pamphlets on women's rights. Finally, in 1843, she enrolled in Oberlin College in Ohio, the only college that would admit women.

Stone dreamed of being a public speaker. Attending public lectures was a popular American pastime. Public lecturers were the celebrities of their day. They toured the country, spreading important ideas and often making good money. At Oberlin, Stone wanted to study oratory (public speaking) and practice debate. Although college officials thought public speaking was inappropriate for women, Stone organized a debating society for female students.

By then Stone was a dedicated abolitionist. At Oberlin—a stop on the Underground Railroad and the first US college to admit black students—she taught escaped slaves to read, and she learned about the horrors of enslavement from them. Shortly after graduation, she got her dream job. The American Anti-Slavery Society hired her to go on a public lecture tour. She brought audiences to tears as she described the suffering of slaves and their brave flights to freedom. A reporter wrote, "I have never, anywhere heard a speaker whose style of eloquence I more admired: the pride of her acquaintants, the idol of the crowd, wherever she goes, the people *en masse* turn out to hear Lucy Stone."

The question of slavery deeply divided the nation, and speaking out against it made some people extremely angry. But Stone could handle herself when things turned rough. At one event on Cape Cod, Massachusetts, an angry mob attacked the platform where Stone was sitting with several colleagues. The crowd grabbed one of the male speakers, tore his coat, and started to beat him. "You'd better run, Stephen," Stone told him.

"But who will take care of you?" he asked.

Stone took the arm of a muscular man who had been threatening the speakers with a club. "This man will take care of me," she said. Talking softly to him, she transformed him from one of the assailants into her own personal bodyguard. The man helped her through the crowd, lifted her up onto a tree stump (which she used as a speaking platform), and used his club to threaten anyone who shouted at her. She not only won over the crowd, but she inspired them to take up a collection to replace her colleague's torn coat.

Over time, Stone began to see a connection between slaves' lack of freedom and women's lack of freedom. She began to talk about that in her speeches. Her boss, Samuel May, told her to stick to the antislavery message. Stone offered her resignation, saying, "I was a woman before I was an abolitionist. I must speak for the women." However, May did not want to lose her. They came to a compromise. Stone would take a decrease in pay and lecture against slavery on the weekends. During the week, she would lecture on women's rights. Stone feared that no one would pay to hear her women's rights lectures. But they proved popular, and soon she was bringing in very good money.

Beyond being an extremely powerful speaker, Stone proved to be a brilliant organizer. In October 1850, she helped organize the first National Women's Rights Convention, held in Worcester, Massachusetts. More than one thousand people attended the convention, and more were turned away due to lack of space. Stone's speech at the convention drew thunderous applause and was reported in newspapers across the Northeast.

Following the convention, Stone continued to lecture. She also took on lobbying efforts—she spoke to lawmakers and tried to convince them to pass laws that were fair to women. She collected signatures on petitions—written requests submitted to public officials—asking for women's property rights and women's right to vote. Wherever she went, she helped women start their own reform groups.

"MORE THAN THE APPENDAGES OF SOCIETY"

Susan Brownell Anthony was born on February 15, 1820, on a farm in Adams, Massachusetts. Her mother, Lucy Read Anthony, was a Baptist. Her father, Daniel Anthony, was a Quaker. The two had grown up on neighboring farms, where they lived very different lives. Baptists were allowed to sing and dance and wear bright colors. Quakers were expected to be somber and quiet, wearing simple gray clothes. Quaker children could not own games or toys, and adults did not decorate their homes. These rules were to ensure that children and adults focused on the inner light, or the spirit of God inside them, rather than on worldly distractions. The Anthonys raised their children as Quakers, with no toys, music, or games.

Susan's father was a financial success. Near the family farm, he opened a factory that manufactured cotton cloth. It was so prosperous that he moved the family to Battenville, New York, where he built a larger factory and the family moved into a large new house. He started a school for the factory workers and their children and paid for many of the buildings in town.

In 1837 the United States suffered an economic crash that led to a depression. Daniel Anthony's businesses went broke. He had to sell the family's house. Susan Anthony left school and took a job as a teacher to help support

her family. By the time she was twenty-six, she was the head of the female department of the prestigious Canajoharie Academy. She earned significantly less than her male counterparts did.

Susan B. Anthony posed for this portrait around 1870. Anthony championed an amendment to the US Constitution that would grant voting rights to women. Her fellow suffragists nicknamed it the Susan B. Anthony Amendment.

In 1853 Anthony attended a state teachers' convention. She was one of three hundred female teachers, all seated in the back of the hall. The two hundred male teachers in attendance sat in the front. Only the men were allowed to speak. One of them raised the question of why teaching was not a more respected profession. Anthony rose to her feet and said, "Mr. President." She wanted to address the conference.

The other teachers were shocked that a woman would speak up in a public place. The men debated for half an hour before finally deciding to let her speak. She then told them, "It seems to me, gentlemen, that none of you quite comprehend the cause of the disrespect of which you complain. Do you not see that so long as society says a woman is incompetent to be a lawyer, minister, or doctor, but has ample ability to be a teacher, that every man of you who chooses this profession tacitly acknowledges that he has no more brains than a woman?" Male teachers were poorly paid, she said, because they had to compete with female teachers, who were paid even less. She argued that showing respect for women's intelligence and insisting that women be paid as much as men would benefit all teachers.

Anthony did not want to be a teacher forever. She did not particularly want to be a wife either. What she most wanted, she finally decided, was to be a reformer. She joined a temperance organization, a group that opposed the drinking of alcohol.

In October 1850, Anthony read a newspaper account of the first National Women's Rights Convention. She was very moved by Lucy Stone's words: "We want to be something more than the appendages of Society; we want that Woman should be coequal and help-meet [helpmate] of Man in all the interest and perils and enjoyments of human life." Forty years later, Anthony credited this speech with first inspiring her to work for women's rights.

A FORMIDABLE TEAM

In 1851 Susan B. Anthony met Elizabeth Cady Stanton through Amelia Bloomer, a mutual friend. Soon the two became great friends and political partners. Anthony connected Stanton to the wider world during the lonely years when Stanton was stuck at home caring for her young children. Stanton was the stronger writer, and Anthony would beg, flatter, and browbeat Stanton into writing lectures for her.

BLOOMERS: THE THINKING-WOMAN'S FASHION

Women's rights activists formed tight bonds with one another. Reforms that seemed good and obvious to them struck most people as ridiculous and immoral. One example was dress reform. During the nineteenth century, women's clothes were uncomfortable and inconvenient. Their long skirts dragged along the ground and picked up dirt. They had to be lifted when going up stairs. Tightly laced corsets restricted women's breathing, and layers of hoops and petticoats beneath skirts

made it difficult to move and sit. Women's clothing reinforced the idea that women were weak, docile, and idle by making it difficult for them to move freely and exercise vigorously.

Stanton's cousin Libby Smith Miller designed a more practical outfit, consisting of loose trousers worn under a knee-length skirt (*left*). Stanton loved the way it made it easier to chase after the children and do housework. She could even carry a baby and a candle up the stairs at the same time! Miller's design became popular when Amelia Bloomer printed a pattern in her temperance newspaper, the *Lily*, in 1852. So people began calling them bloomers.

The comfort and convenience of bloomers came at a cost. Lucy Stone described going to the post office in New York with Susan B. Anthony, both wearing bloomers: "Gradually we noticed that we were being encircled. A wall of men and boys at last shut us in, so that to go on or to go back was impossible. There we stood. The crowd was a good-natured one. They laughed at us. They made faces at us. They said impertinent things, and they would not let us out. Every moment brought added numbers, who peered over to see what attracted the crowd." Finally, a friend went for a police officer, who broke up the crowd.

Female reformers had enough trouble being taken seriously, without the added distraction of unusual clothes. One by one, they went back to wearing traditional dress, at least in public. Elizabeth Cady Stanton continued to wear bloomers around the house.

At times, Anthony even provided help around the house to make Stanton's work possible. In 1856 Anthony implored, "So for the love of me and for the saving of the reputation of womanhood, I beg you, with one baby on your knee and another at your feet, and four boys whistling, buzzing, hallooing 'Ma, Ma,' set yourself about the work [of writing]."

Stanton replied, "Come here and I will do what I can . . . if you will hold the baby and make the puddings."

Anthony was close friends with Lucy Stone as well. They often traveled together on lecture tours and helped each other organize petition drives and plan conventions. They filled their letters with pledges of love and loyalty to each other. They also pledged their loyalty to the cause of women's rights. However, the friendship deteriorated after Lucy Stone got married. Stone had long believed she would never marry. Her parents' unhappy relationship and her father's cruelty did not provide a hopeful example of marriage. She also hated the thought of giving a husband complete control over her body, her property, and any children she might have.

When she was thirty-five years old, Henry (Harry) Blackwell entered the picture. He was visiting Boston from Cincinnati. His sister took him to listen as Stone gave testimony to the Massachusetts state legislature. She spoke eloquently for a proposed women's rights amendment to the state constitution. Blackwell was impressed and set out to meet her, thinking she might make a good wife. When they did meet several months later, he proposed marriage immediately.

Stone was astonished. Blackwell was an impulsive, charming, and ambitious man, and they shared many views. Like Stone, he opposed slavery, approved of temperance, and favored women's rights. His sisters Elizabeth and Emily Blackwell were two of the first female doctors in the United States. Stone knew of his sisters and admired their reputations, but she was not about to marry a man she had only just met. Stone eventually fell in love with Blackwell and agreed to marry him, but she did not want to lose her independence or her rights. The couple wrote their objections to the current laws of marriage, saying that they would not obey any laws that "refuse to recognize the wife as an independent, rational being, while they confer upon the husband an injurious and unnatural superiority." The minister read their protest as part of the marriage ceremony. Lucy Stone never took her husband's name. To be sure that no one mistakenly called her Lucy Stone Blackwell, she signed her letters, "Lucy Stone (Only)."

CONFLICTING COMMITMENTS

Marriage was not an easy transition for Stone. Her relationship with Blackwell failed to fully live up to their goals for equality. Even while Stone was away earning money on a speaking tour, Blackwell wrote to scold her for not mending his leggings. Lucy found it difficult to balance married life with her reform work.

In 1857, at the age of thirty-nine, Lucy Stone gave birth to a daughter, Alice Stone Blackwell. She had only one other child, a boy who died at birth. For the next ten years, Stone devoted herself to motherhood, giving up most of her reform activities.

Lucy Stone was not the only leader of the woman's rights movement to follow this pattern. Antoinette Brown Blackwell, one of Stone's closest friends and the first woman to be ordained as a mainstream Protestant minister, also cut down on her suffrage work to start a family.

Susan B. Anthony felt abandoned and overworked. She complained, "Those of you who have talent to do honor to poor—oh how poor—womanhood have all given yourselves over to baby-making; and left poor . . . me to do battle alone."

Stanton counseled patience. She wrote to Anthony, "Let Lucy and Antionette rest awhile in peace and quietness and think great thoughts for the future. It is not well to be in the excitement of public life all the time; do not keep stirring them up or mourning over their repose. You need rest too, Susan. Let the world alone awhile. We cannot bring about a moral revolution in a day or a year."

3

DASHED HOPES AND BROKEN BONDS

In the mid-nineteenth century, the United States was becoming ever more divided over the issue of slavery. Many white Americans were moving to the West, populating territories that would eventually become states. Politicians fought bitterly about whether slavery would be legal in those new states. Violent clashes sprang up between opponents and supporters of slavery in Kansas Territory and other parts of the nation.

In 1860 tensions came to a head with the election of Abraham Lincoln as US president. Although Lincoln had not called for the complete abolition of slavery, he was opposed to adding any new slave states. And as a member of the antislavery Republican Party, he was unacceptable to many southerners. On December 20, 1860, South Carolina seceded (withdrew) from the United States. Over the next several months, six more southern states seceded. They argued that the federal government did not respect their rights as states to determine their own laws. They declared themselves a new nation: the Confederate States of America.

On April 12, 1861, federal troops clashed with Confederate forces at Fort Sumter in South Carolina, beginning the Civil War. Lincoln called on all states to send men to join the army. Four more states seceded rather than send troops.

Harriet Beecher Stowe (*left*) wrote the novel *Uncle Tom's Cabin* (1852) to dramatize the horrors of slavery and boost support for abolition. The debate over slavery ultimately led to the US Civil War.

For the next four years, a bloody war between the Union (North) and the Confederacy (South) consumed the nation.

During the Civil War, most suffrage work stopped. Suffragists—based mostly in the North—focused on supporting Union soldiers and ending slavery. Susan B. Anthony thought it was a mistake to give up on suffrage work during the war. She was afraid women would lose ground if they didn't keep pushing for the vote. But other suffragists believed that the country's leaders would see that women were organized, capable, and patriotic citizens. They thought the government would reward them with the vote once the war was over.

In 1863 Lincoln issued the Emancipation Proclamation, which freed slaves in the Confederate states. The proclamation theoretically freed more than 3.5 million of the nation's 4 million slaves. But since it applied only to the Confederate states, which were actively at war with the federal government, it was difficult to enforce. The proclamation did not outlaw slavery or give freed slaves (called freedmen) citizenship.

Abolitionists wanted to pass an amendment to the US Constitution that would end slavery completely and permanently. Many suffragists campaigned for the Thirteenth Amendment, which says that "neither slavery nor involuntary servitude, except as punishment for crime whereof the party shall have been duly convicted, shall exist within the United States, or any place subject to their jurisdiction."

On May 13, 1865, the Confederate forces surrendered, and the Thirteenth Amendment became law on December 6, 1865, freeing the last of the nation's slaves. The war had been horrific, costing at least 620,000 lives. But when it was over, reformers believed that the United States would become a more just and equal country—one in which both blacks and women could vote.

"THIS HOUR BELONGS TO THE NEGRO"

In 1866 Susan B. Anthony, Elizabeth Cady Stanton, Lucy Stone, and the women of the Eleventh Annual National Women's Rights Convention formed the American Equal Rights Association. They vowed to fight "to secure Equal Rights to all American citizens, especially the right of suffrage, irrespective of race, color or sex." Lucretia Mott was elected president, and Frederick Douglass became one of the group's vice presidents.

Anthony, Stone, and Stanton were also members of the American Anti-Slavery Society. With slavery abolished, William Lloyd Garrison, founder and president of the society, thought the organization should be dissolved. But the majority of members

"THE BOOK THAT MADE THIS GREAT WAR"

In 1852 the novel *Uncle Tom's Cabin*, written by Harriet Beecher Stowe, brought the horrors of slavery to life for northern readers. Inspired by the memoir of Josiah Henson, an escaped slave, the book details the hardships experienced by Uncle Tom, a middle-aged slave who has been sold away from his wife and family. Another main character in the book is a young slave mother named Eliza, who runs away to prevent her child from being sold.

According to Stowe family legend, when Lincoln met Harriet Beecher Stowe during a visit to the White House in 1862, he exclaimed, "So you're the little woman who wrote the book that made this great war!" In all likelihood, Lincoln never actually said those words, but the book did have a huge impact on the nation. It drove antislavery sentiment in the North and incited fury in the South. *Uncle Tom's Cabin* was the second best-selling book in the United States during the nineteenth century, after the Bible. Later, some people criticized the book for promoting racial stereotypes and using offensive terms to describe African Americans.

Former slave Frederick Douglass was a leader in the American abolition and women's suffrage movements. After the Thirteenth Amendment (1865) to the US Constitution abolished slavery in the United States, Douglass worked to secure voting rights for black men.

disagreed. They thought that their job was not finished until black men had the right to vote. So Garrison left the organization, and Wendell Phillips became the new president.

Anthony, Stone, and Stanton suggested that the society merge with the American Equal Rights Association. That way, reformers could save time, energy, and money by working for both black suffrage and woman suffrage. Phillips declined. The women were surprised, because Phillips had long supported women's rights. He had argued vigorously for seating the women delegates at the 1840 World Anti-Slavery Convention, where Stanton and Mott had met. But he believed that asking for woman suffrage and black suffrage at the same time was too risky. Phillips told the women they must focus on one question at a time and said, "This hour belongs to the Negro [a commonly used term for African Americans at this time]." His focus was on securing voting rights for black men.

Phillips thought that though women and black men equally deserved the vote, black men needed it more. Four million black men and black women had only recently been freed from slavery. Their situation was extremely perilous. They had no money, no land, no jobs, and no education. Most of them lived in the South, where their former masters and other white people looked on them with hatred and anger. In many southern cities, angry white mobs attacked black citizens, killing, raping, and burning homes. Similar incidents also happened in New York and other northern cities. Phillips said that black men needed to be able to vote for officials who would protect them, their rights, and their families.

Stanton, Anthony, and Stone were outraged. Susan B. Anthony told Phillips that she would rather cut off her right hand than ask for the ballot for black men and not for women too. To ask women to wait for the vote, putting black men first, seemed unjust and unnecessary. Lucy Stone thought women were being asked to accept "the poor half loaf of justice for the Negro, poisoned by its lack of justice for every woman of the land."

Stanton, Anthony, and Stone felt betrayed. But their outrage brought to the surface underlying racism. Stanton made it very clear that she did not think uneducated and "degraded" former slaves should be making laws for her to obey. She argued that educated white women like herself would make much better political decisions than former slaves would. She also said that immigrant men, such as poorly educated Germans and Irishmen, were less qualified to vote than well-educated, American-born white women were. She argued for educated suffrage—that only the most intelligent and well-educated people (men *and* women) should be allowed to vote.

How did black women feel about this debate? Amid the violence and chaos following the Civil War, the vast majority of newly freed black women in the South were concerned with basic survival—ensuring that their families were safe and fed. Sojourner Truth, a hero of the abolition movement, had been born a slave in New York State, had been freed when New York banned slavery in 1828, and had worked for years assisting slaves who had escaped from the South. Truth actively supported woman suffrage and worried that black women would remain vulnerable if only black men got the vote. She said at an American Equal Rights Association meeting, at which black participants were welcomed, "There is a great stir about colored [black] men getting their rights, but not a word about the colored women, and if colored men get their rights, and not colored women theirs, you see the colored men will be masters over the women and it will be just as bad as it was before."

Frances Ellen Watkins Harper had a somewhat different view. She was one of the few black women members of the association. Born free in Baltimore, Maryland, in 1825, she was a gifted poet whose first book of poems was published when she was twenty. Before the Civil War, she had participated in the Underground Railroad and been a public speaker for the American Anti-Slavery Society. After the Civil

War, she gave lectures supporting black men's right to vote. She focused especially on the nearly two hundred thousand black men who had fought for the North during the Civil War, arguing that they deserved the vote in return for their service. Though she supported universal suffrage—voting rights for all—Harper tended to be sympathetic to the claim that black men needed the vote more urgently than women did.

"AIN'T I A WOMAN?"

In 1851 Sojourner Truth (*below right*) attended a woman's rights convention in Akron, Ohio. A white male minister there argued that women were delicate creatures who needed stronger, smarter men to protect them and take care of them. Truth stood up and reminded the group that not all women were coddled and protected. While in upper-class white society, men might help women into carriages and lift them over ditches, black women had no such assistance. As a slave in New York, Truth had plowed fields, planted crops, and done other backbreaking farmwork. She had worked as hard as a man, ate as much food as a man—when she could get it—and tolerated the whippings of the overseers as well as a man. "And ain't I a woman?" she demanded. "I have born thirteen children, and seen them most all sold off to slavery, and when I cried out with my mother's grief, none but Jesus heard me. And ain't I a woman?" Truth's speech was heralded at the time and ever since as one of the greatest claims for women's equality in the United States.

CATASTROPHE IN KANSAS

In 1867 the Republican-controlled Kansas legislature passed two measures that needed voter approval to become law. One measure would remove the word *white* from the list of voter qualifications. The other would remove the word *male*. If both passed, all adult citizens of Kansas would be able to vote, regardless of race or sex. But if only the first referendum passed, it would show that voters there supported black men's suffrage more than woman suffrage. That would strengthen the argument that combining them would hurt black men's chances. So suffragists saw Kansas as an important test case.

Lucy Stone and her husband went to Kansas in the spring to campaign for both measures. Based on their reception, they realized that they needed to do a lot more work or neither measure would pass on Election Day that November. The American Equal Rights Association hired thirty-two-year-old Olympia Brown, an ordained Universalist minister and experienced woman suffrage speaker, to canvass the state. Susan B. Anthony and Elizabeth Cady Stanton hoped to go to Kansas as well, as soon as they could raise enough money to cover their travel expenses.

While the Republican Party, which had grown out of the antislavery movement in 1854, generally supported black suffrage, Kansas Republicans split over woman suffrage. One faction supported it, but another group campaigned against it. Opponents of woman suffrage heaped abuse and intimidation on Brown and her local allies. They said that suffragists were dishonest, mannish, and sexually promiscuous. Meanwhile, the Democrats in Kansas were firmly against black suffrage and did all they could to sabotage that cause. They printed articles claiming that black men in the South were refusing to work, stealing anything they could get their hands on, and demanding to marry white women.

Kansans who opposed both measures deliberately tried to drive a wedge between black suffragists and woman suffragists. They published newspaper reports of each side criticizing the other. Historians believe that at least some of these reports were made up. Nevertheless, it was true that the two campaigns did not work together well nor trust each other.

To increase cooperation, Olympia Brown and black suffrage campaigner

Woodson Twine launched joint meetings. There they each argued for both black and woman suffrage. But the negative reports and the sabotage continued.

When Stanton and Anthony finally arrived in Kansas, they spoke strongly for both causes. Yet they had limited support from reform organizations in the East and from the Republican Party. Their opponents kept up a barrage of negative press and harassment. Prospects in Kansas looked bleak.

Two weeks before the election, George Francis Train entered the fray. A wealthy entrepreneur and independent candidate for president, Train was willing to give both time and money to the women's cause. Train didn't just give lectures. He put on a show. He was funny and fast-talking, did dead-on impersonations, acted out vignettes, and composed satirical poetry off the top of his head. People flocked to see him.

Train was also an unabashed racist. Before the Civil War, he had defended slavery, claiming that it instilled the values of white society in black people, whom he called an inferior race. In supporting woman suffrage, Train repeatedly argued that white women were more qualified and deserving of the vote than black men. His viewpoint angered the leaders of the black suffrage campaign. Anthony and Stanton not only accepted Train's help, but they traveled with him for the final two weeks of the campaign, implicitly supporting his racist views.

Both causes lost by a landslide. Only 9,070 white males cast their votes for woman suffrage, while 19,857 voted against it. For black suffrage, the numbers were 10,483 votes for it and 19,421 against it. Most voters either supported both measures or rejected both. Few supported only black suffrage or only women suffrage.

The twin defeats in Kansas weakened and fractured the American Equal Rights Association. Anthony and Stanton's alliance with Train appalled many of their friends. Stone turned her back when Anthony tried to introduce her to Train. But by then, Anthony and Stanton were willing to take any help. Train expanded their audiences, helping them reach working-class men and women who had never come to an abolition or woman's rights lecture before. He also offered funds to start a newspaper, which they enthusiastically accepted. The Revolution ran from 1868 to 1872, until Train's money ran out and Anthony was $10,000 in debt.

WHITE TERROR

Reconstruction (1865–1877) was a US government plan for readmitting Confederate states into the Union following the Civil War. It was also set up to help former enslaved Americans integrate into free society in the South. Reconstruction included a series of legislative actions, including the Fourteenth Amendment to the US Constitution. Passed in 1868, the amendment was designed to ensure that former slaves had the rights of full US citizens, with equal protection under the law. The amendment also punished states (by decreasing the number of representatives in the US Congress) if they did not give all male citizens over the age of twenty-one the right to vote. Other Reconstruction laws required southern states to adopt new constitutions, guaranteeing voting rights for black men, and to elect new state leaders. Those states that met all the requirements of Reconstruction were allowed back into the Union.

To enforce the new laws, the federal government sent soldiers to southern states. And thousands of northerners moved to the South to work as teachers, missionaries, business owners, and politicians. These so-called carpetbaggers (named for their fabric suitcases) voted Republican. So did blacks and the small number of white southerners (called *scalawags*, a word meaning "rascals") who supported Reconstruction. But many other southerners, appalled by the prospect of black men voting, refused to vote in protest. Some southern white men—former Confederate officials or military officers—were barred from voting or holding office by Reconstruction laws. Together, carpetbaggers, blacks, and scalawags elected Republican governments throughout the South, including many black lawmakers.

Republican control did not last long in the South. Reconstruction infuriated many white southerners, who were determined to take back their state governments and to strip black people of their new rights. Just after the war, in about 1865 or 1866, a secret society called the Ku Klux Klan formed in Tennessee. Donning masks and white robes, members used violence and threats against black people and their allies to maintain white supremacy in the South. Between 1866 and 1871, the Klan murdered hundreds of black people and injured thousands more. Klan members burned down black people's houses, churches, and schools; hunted down blacks and killed them by hanging; and drove black farmers off their land. On October 22, 1868, a Klan member shot and killed James M. Hinds, a white Republican congressional representative from Arkansas. The terror and violence kept so many Republicans, black and white, from voting that the Democrats retook power in Louisiana and Georgia.

A RANCOROUS SPLIT

In this volatile atmosphere, the American Equal Rights Association had a fateful meeting on May 12, 1869. First up for discussion was the proposed Fifteenth Amendment to the US Constitution. The amendment says, "The right of citizens of the United States to vote shall not be denied or abridged by the United States or by any state on account of race, color, or previous condition of servitude."The amendment was designed to protect the voting rights of black men. Elizabeth Cady Stanton and Susan B. Anthony argued that the association should oppose the amendment because it did not include women.

Frederick Douglass had always been a strong supporter of woman suffrage and was a friend to Elizabeth Cady Stanton. But he disapproved of the racist language Stanton had been using, and he diplomatically told her so. He also vividly outlined the dangers facing black men in the nation, explaining that for them, attaining the ballot was a matter of life and death. At the meeting, he said,

> When women, because they are women, are hunted down through the cities of New York and New Orleans; when they are dragged from their houses and hung upon lamp-posts; when their children are torn from their arms, and their brains dashed out upon the pavement; when they are objects of insult and outrage at every turn; when they are in danger of having their homes burnt down over their heads; when their children are not allowed to enter schools; then they will have an urgency to obtain the ballot equal to our own.

An audience member asked, "Is that not all true about black women?"

Douglass replied, "Yes, yes, yes; it is true of the black woman, but not because she is a woman, but because she is black."

Susan B. Anthony was not convinced. If suffrage was not for all people, she insisted, it should be given to white women before black men. She told the meeting, "If intelligence, justice, and morality are to have precedence in the Government, let the question of woman be brought up first, and that of the negro last."

Lucy Stone tried to smooth things over by arguing that each side had a point. She rejected Douglass's assertion that women were better off than black men, saying, "Woman has [to endure] an ocean of wrongs too deep for any to plummet, and the negro too, has [to endure] an ocean of wrongs that cannot be fathomed." She came out in support of the Fifteenth Amendment, thanking God for it and hoping it would be passed in every state. (Under the US Constitution, three-quarters of the states must ratify an amendment for it to become law.) But she ended by saying, "I believe that the safety of the government would be more promoted by the admission of woman as an element of restoration and harmony than the negro. I believe that the influence of women will save the country before every other power."

Finally, Frances Harper had a chance to speak. She said that she prioritized racial equality ahead of equality between the sexes. White women, however, had the opposite priority, and she questioned whether they really welcomed black women into their alliance. She ended by saying, as paraphrased in the meeting's official report, "If the nation could only handle one question [I] would not have the black woman put a single straw in the way, if only the men of the race could obtain what they wanted."

Unable to come to an agreement about its priorities, the American Equal Rights Association dissolved. That very evening, Anthony and Stanton formed a new organization: the National Woman Suffrage Association. Blaming men for the split within the American Equal Rights Association, the two women decided not to allow males in their organization and to work for woman suffrage and nothing else. One of their first acts was to condemn the Fifteenth Amendment as supporting an "aristocracy of sex."

Soon thereafter, Lucy Stone and her allies formed a rival suffrage association. The American Woman Suffrage Association supported the Fifteenth Amendment. This group allowed men to be members and officers.

The Fifteenth Amendment became law in 1870. But it failed to provide racial equality. Only seven years later, Reconstruction collapsed in utter failure. Because of worsening economic conditions and frustration with Reconstruction, Americans voted the Republicans out of power. In 1877 the US Army pulled out of the South and all efforts to impose racial equality ended. Free of what they viewed as northern interference, southern whites instituted the Jim Crow system of segregation. Through a combination of laws and social customs, black Americans could not share public facilities such as train cars, schools, restaurants, theaters, parks, and cemeteries with whites.

According to the Fifteenth Amendment, states could not pass laws that explicitly barred black men from voting. So instead, many southern states imposed poll taxes and literacy tests. Poll taxes were fees that voters had to pay before casting ballots. Early poll taxes were one or two dollars, then the equivalent of at least two week's wages for most people. Recently freed slaves were almost all poor. The government had granted them freedom but very little else. So most black people could not afford to pay the tax. And since most blacks had been denied schooling, most could not read and pass literacy tests. These problems—along with threats and violence—made it all but impossible for black men in the South to vote.

The federal government did nothing to stop these unfair voting practices. And despite their avowed support for the Fifteenth Amendment, the American Woman Suffrage Association did nothing to challenge them either.

4

UNEASY ALLIES

Strategies for winning the vote for women continued to shift. The American Woman Suffrage Association under Lucy Stone chose a step-by-step approach. It supported local efforts to win limited voting rights for women, often starting with school board elections. Voting for the school board arguably fit into women's role as mothers, so people had an easier time accepting the idea. It was also easier to get through the legislature. Enfranchising women in all state elections generally required changing a state's constitution. This was difficult, often requiring approval by two-thirds of both chambers of the state legislature (the house and the senate). Voters also had to approve the change. Enfranchising women for school board elections required only a majority (more than half of the votes) in the state legislature. Suffragists also fought for the ballot (the right to vote) in western territories (areas that had not yet become states). And they fought for it in city, state, and presidential elections in many states.

This piece-by-piece approach was extremely time-consuming, expensive, and frustrating. There were many losses, even in lower-stakes campaigns. So Anthony and Stanton's National Woman Suffrage Association preferred to focus on amending the federal constitution. The goal of that approach would be to enfranchise women throughout the country in one step. They proposed what they hoped would be the Sixteenth Amendment, modeled on the Fifteenth: "The right of

When she married Henry Blackwell in 1855, suffragist Lucy Stone refused to change her name to Blackwell. Women who followed her lead and kept their maiden names were called Lucy Stoners. This photo of Stone dates to the 1860s.

citizens of the United States to vote shall not be denied or abridged [limited] by the United States or by any State on account of sex."

Suffragists lobbied intensively, but Congress refused to vote on the amendment. As the United States adopted other, unrelated amendments, it became clear that woman suffrage would never be the Sixteenth or the Seventeenth or even the Eighteenth Amendment. With its future unknown, advocates called it the Susan B. Anthony Amendment.

NEW DEPARTURE, NEW HOPE

While suffragists debated a federal amendment versus a state-by-state approach, a few legal scholars argued for an easier way. They believed that the Fourteenth Amendment, if interpreted correctly, already gave women the right to vote. The amendment said that no state could deny any citizen the rights granted by federal law. And since all people born in the United States (including women) were citizens and voting was a right of citizenship, then women could not be denied the vote. The husband-and-wife team Francis and Virginia Minor of Missouri (he was a lawyer; she was the leader of Missouri's suffrage movement) were the first to set out this argument, in 1869. They used it to sue a government official who refused to allow Virginia Minor to register to vote. While the Minors' case made its way through the courts, their argument got a much more colorful and controversial advocate in Victoria Claflin Woodhull.

Victoria Claflin was born into a poor Ohio family in 1838. Her mother told fortunes. Her father was a con man who sold fake medical treatments. At the age of fifteen, Victoria married Canning Woodhull, an unscrupulous doctor twice her age. Woodhull was an alcoholic and an unfaithful husband. When she was twenty-eight years old, she left him for her second husband, James Harvey Blood. She kept Woodhull as her last name.

Victoria Woodhull was a smart, ambitious, and multitalented woman. She and her sister Tennessee (Tennie) Claflin earned good money as psychics and magnetic healers. They claimed to cure people using the magnetic forces in their hands. In the 1870s, the sisters became spiritualists. Spiritualism was a nineteenth-century religious movement, popular in suffragist circles. Spiritualists believed that certain individuals, often young women, could hear messages from the dead. At a time when most families had lost loved ones to illness or war, spiritualism offered a connection between the living and their dead loved ones. Victoria Woodhull talked to various spirits and claimed particular connections with the ancient Greek orator Demosthenes, and with the French emperor Napoleon Bonaparte and his wife Empress Josephine.

PASSING A CONSTITUTIONAL AMENDMENT

Before it can become part of the US Constitution, a proposed amendment must go through a challenging approval process. It must first win at least two-thirds of the votes in both the US House of Representatives and the US Senate. Three-fourths of the states must ratify, or approve, it.

States set their own policies for ratifying amendments. Some state legislatures first send amendments to a committee. This subset of legislators must approve an amendment before it is voted on by the legislature. Most states require approval of the proposed amendment by a majority (more than 50 percent of the vote) in both houses of the state legislature.

Through spiritualism the sisters met New Yorker Cornelius Vanderbilt, one of the wealthiest men in the world. Vanderbilt liked to consult the spirits for advice on both personal and business matters. He was grateful for business tips he received from Victoria Woodhull. (She received some of her information from friends who were romantically involved with Vanderbilt's business rivals, rather than from spirits.) Vanderbilt also developed a romantic relationship with Tennie Claflin, who treated him for his aches and pains with magnetic healing.

Vanderbilt owned steamship lines and railroads. He put up money for the sisters to start a Wall Street brokerage firm—a business that buys and sells stocks. The novelty of a female-owned stock brokerage attracted lots of press and plenty of clients, including a number of women. With the help of Vanderbilt and Blood, the sisters made a fortune dealing in stocks. The sisters also started a newspaper. *Woodhull & Claflin's Weekly* published on a variety of topics, including spiritualism, vegetarianism, and woman suffrage.

Woodhull had almost no formal schooling. Yet she was extremely bright and had an incredible memory. In January 1871, she became the first woman to address a committee of the US Congress. Her friend Representative Benjamin Butler of Massachusetts had invited her. She presented a memorial (an argument to a government) for woman suffrage to the joint House and Senate Judiciary Committee. Her argument drew on the Fourteenth and Fifteenth Amendments as well as other parts of the Constitution. She asked Congress to clarify that women already had the right to vote under these laws. Butler likely wrote the document, although Woodhull later claimed that spirits had dictated it to her. After a hesitant start, Woodhull presented her memorial with passion and conviction.

Woodhull and her memorial did not impress most of the Judiciary Committee. But Susan B. Anthony and other National Woman Suffrage Association leaders *were* impressed. They were excited by Woodhull's arguments, which Stanton called a "new departure." They were also impressed with Woodhull. She was young and beautiful, with an intensity and confidence that were compelling. She also had a great deal of money, which the suffrage cause needed.

Anthony called her a "bright, glorious, young and strong spirit" and said she had brought new life and hope to the suffrage movement.

"A FIRST VOTE ALMOST"

Using the Fourteenth/Fifteenth Amendment argument (the "new departure"), more than one hundred women in ten states tried to register to vote in 1871 and 1872. One of these was Mary Ann Shadd Cary, an African American woman who had been born free in Wilmington, Delaware. That state did not allow black children to be educated, so her family moved to Pennsylvania so Mary Ann and her siblings could go to school. As a young woman, she moved to Canada, where she helped escaped slaves and ran a newspazper, the *Provincial Freeman.* She also married and had two children. During the Civil War, Cary returned to the United States to recruit black men to join the Union army. After the war, she taught the children of freed slaves in Washington, DC, and got her law degree from Howard University School of Law. (Howard is a historically black university that was established in 1867 for black students.)

Cary supported the National Woman Suffrage Association from its beginning, despite its sometimes racist rhetoric. She greatly admired Susan B. Anthony and Elizabeth Cady Stanton and encouraged them to include black women in their suffrage efforts. She was also fully behind the new departure. So, on April 14, 1871, Cary tried to register to vote in Washington, DC. All around her were jubilant black men, registering to vote for the first time. Some of these men encouraged her and praised her courage. Others were not supportive. One man said she ought to be whipped for attempting to vote. The registration board refused to allow Cary to register. Disappointed, she went home and wrote a newspaper article "A First Vote Almost." She said that the refusal "was and is a bitter pill to swallow."

One year later, Susan B. Anthony had slightly more success. She and fourteen other women registered to vote in their hometown of Rochester, New York, on November 1, 1872. Four days later, the women returned to cast their ballots in the presidential election. Anthony voted a straight Republican ticket, including a vote for Ulysses S. Grant for president. However, a few weeks later, the police arrested and charged the women with voting illegally. Anthony insisted that the deputy marshal arrest her by putting her in handcuffs—as a man would have been. After being released on bail (paying a fee and promising to return for a court hearing), she spoke in Rochester before her trial about woman suffrage and the new departure.

Before the women's trial, the judge decided Anthony had prejudiced potential jurors through her talks. So he moved the trial to a different county where people were less likely to know about her. In response, Anthony and fellow suffragist Matilda Joslyn Gage went to that county, visiting one village each day to talk about the rationale for the new departure. Anthony's eventual trial was a sham. She had requested to speak in her own defense, which the judge would not allow because Anthony was a woman. Nor did he allow the jury to decide the case. He issued a guilty verdict himself before sentencing Anthony to pay a fine of one hundred dollars. She swore she would never pay it, and she never did. The judge could have had her imprisoned for refusing to pay. But he did not want her to attract more publicity by appealing the case to a higher court, so he let the matter drop.

By 1875 Virginia Minor's voting rights case, *Minor v. Happersett,* had reached the US Supreme Court. The court ruled against her, stating that the Fourteenth Amendment did not give women the right to vote. This and another similar court case killed the new departure as a suffrage strategy.

FREE LOVE FALLOUT

Meanwhile, Victoria Woodhull was using her newfound fame to further her political ambitions. She had long wanted to run for president of the United States. In 1872 she started her own political party—the Equal Rights Party—and it nominated her for president. (It also nominated Frederick Douglass for vice president, without his knowledge or consent. He later declined the nomination.) In this way, Woodhull became the first woman to run for president of the United States.

Woodhull did not meet the minimum age requirement of thirty-five. She was too young by a few months. As far as the press was concerned, however, Woodhull's age was less of an issue than her support for free love. Free love was the idea that love and sexual relations should not be controlled by the government, the church, or any other institution. Woodhull believed that too many women were trapped in marriages with men who were abusive, alcoholic, unfaithful, or cruel. She believed marriage should be based on love and should last only as long as the two people in it remained

Victoria Woodhull brought new energy to the suffrage movement, although her advocacy of sexual freedom scandalized many Americans.

in love. She said that people should be allowed to marry, divorce, and remarry as often as they pleased and to have sex outside of marriage.

This was a radical idea at the time. American society frowned on divorce. Divorce laws varied widely from state to state. Some states made it virtually impossible for couples to divorce. Others allowed divorce on the grounds of infidelity or abuse but allowed individual judges to determine what constituted abuse. Many judges refused to dissolve marriages if a husband beat his wife. In some states, people could not marry again after divorce, and a few states required each divorce to be voted on by the state legislature.

Society expected both men and women to remain faithful to their spouses. If they did not, men were much more likely to be forgiven for cheating than women were. Divorced women and women who had had affairs often became social outcasts. They were seen as moral failures. In the nineteenth-century worldview, a virtuous woman was an obedient, loyal, and faithful wife, regardless of what her husband did or how he treated her.

The press reported that Woodhull was living with both her ex-husband and her current husband. She explained that her first husband was in poor health and needed her care. But Americans were scandalized. Pushed to declare whether she supported free love only in theory or whether she practiced it, Woodhull finally said, "Yes! I am a free lover! I have an inalienable, constitutional, and natural right to love whom I may, to love as long or as short a period as I can, to change that lover every day if I please!"

Woodhull caused an even greater sensation when she published a detailed account of an extramarital affair between Henry Ward Beecher, a famous and beloved minister, and his parishioner Elizabeth Tilton. Both Beecher and the Tiltons were prominently involved in the women's movement. The so-called "scandal issue" of the *Woodhull & Claflin's Weekly* sold out within hours. Some purchasers rented their ten-cent copies for a dollar a day. One copy sold for forty dollars. The account was so detailed that Woodhull, her husband, and her sister Tennie were jailed on charges of obscenity. When Election Day arrived, Woodhull could not vote for herself for president. She was in jail awaiting trial.

Woodhull's obscenity case was eventually dismissed. She divorced her second husband and moved to England, where she spent the rest of her life. The suffragists were not sorry to see her go. Because of Victoria Woodhull and her connection to free love, more conservative women dropped out of suffrage organizations in droves. Critics said she had set the movement back twenty years. For decades afterward, hecklers accused suffragists of being free lovers. To try to lessen the damage, most suffragists stopped addressing divorce and marriage reform. They saw that for the time being, the issues harmed the larger mission of gaining the right to vote.

"WOMAN WILL BLESS AND BRIGHTEN EVERY PLACE SHE ENTERS"

Suffragists gained another controversial and very different ally in Frances Willard, the charismatic leader of the Woman's Christian Temperance Union (WCTU). Born in 1839, Frank, as she preferred to be called, grew up on the prairies of Wisconsin. She ran wild and free, climbing trees, shooting guns and arrows, and trying to do everything her older brother did. She had no interest in learning to cook, clean, and sew, as her younger sister did. Her mother allowed her to have her way until she was sixteen years old. Then her mother forced her to wear long skirts and corsets and put her hair up "in woman-fashion, twisted up like a corkscrew." The skirts were so heavy that Frank could hardly walk, much less run or climb.

Girls in Frank's day were taught to be modest and unassuming. But young Frank Willard was extraordinarily ambitious. She wrote in her autobiography, "I never knew what it was not to aspire, and not believe myself capable of heroism. I always wanted

Frances Willard headed the Woman's Christian Temperance Union from 1879 to 1898. Many women belonged to both the temperance (anti-alcohol) movement and the suffrage movement. They wanted the right to vote in part so they could vote for bans on the manufacture and sale of alcohol.

to react upon the world about me to my utmost ounce of power, to be widely known and loved and believed in—the more widely the better."

Willard became a teacher, and by 1871, she was dean of Evanston College for Ladies near Chicago, Illinois. She loved the job and was proud of being the first woman to hold such a position. Three years later, the Ladies College became part of Northwestern University. Willard became the dean of women and a professor of English. The president of Northwestern was Charles Fowler, a man she had been briefly engaged to years before. Willard and Fowler argued constantly about how Willard should do her job. Finally, in 1874, she resigned.

At the age of thirty-five, Willard needed a new calling. One fateful day, she came upon a group of women praying and singing hymns in front of a saloon. Willard had stumbled upon a temperance crusade. All over the country, women opposed to the selling and drinking of alcohol were going into saloons to sing hymns and pray. Saloon owners and patrons were so uncomfortable that some saloons shut their doors. The women would then roll the barrels of beer, wine, and liquor into the street and smash them with hatchets. Between December 1873 and November 1874, somewhere between 57,000 and 143,000 women closed thirty thousand US saloons, sometimes for a few days and sometimes for weeks or even months. Many saloons reopened once the crusade had died down.

The temperance movement arose in response to a rise in alcoholism in the nineteenth century. In the early nineteenth century, improved distillation made it cheaper and easier to make strong spirits. Rum from the West Indies and American whiskey from southern states flooded the country. Both liquors were much stronger than the beer and hard cider Americans were used to drinking. The average American adult consumed between 6 and 7 gallons (23 to 26 L) of alcohol per year in 1810. By 1820 average consumption had risen to 7 to 10 gallons (26 to 38 L).

Men were much more likely to drink alcohol than women were. Women were barred from drinking in public, so saloons catered only to men. Public drunkenness and other alcohol-fueled problems were therefore associated with men. Temperance societies noted that alcohol and alcoholism enticed some men to spend too much money in saloons, to drink rather than work, and to neglect and abuse their wives and children.

The first women's temperance society in the United States was founded in 1805. By 1848 the Daughters of Temperance had thirty thousand members, including Susan B. Anthony. Frances Willard had seen the destructiveness of alcoholism firsthand. Her brother Oliver Willard was an alcoholic, and she and her mother were largely responsible for taking care of his wife and children when he could not. When she happened upon the temperance crusaders in Chicago in 1874, she was inspired to join them.

When Willard took action, she moved fast. Within a month, she had joined and become president of the Chicago Temperance Union. She was present at the founding of the WCTU later that year and soon became the new organization's corresponding secretary. Within five years, she was its president.

Under Willard, the WCTU grew. Membership jumped from fourteen thousand in 1879 to seventy thousand in 1885. Willard had outstanding organizational abilities, incredible speaking skills—and personal charisma. She drummed up much of the membership herself on her speaking tours. She gave an average of 365 lectures a year from 1874 to 1883. The WCTU recruited many new members through Protestant churches. Its close association with these churches gave it respectability and made political activism safe and attractive for relatively conservative women.

In its early years, the WCTU focused on persuading people to sign pledges to refrain from drinking. Willard expanded the mission of the organization considerably. Willard viewed alcoholism as not just a personal failing but as a societal ill. (In the nineteenth century, alcoholism was not yet viewed as a disease.) She believed that the causes of drinking were numerous and had to be addressed. So Willard adopted a "Do Everything" approach.

The WCTU pressured states to require temperance education in schools. It fought for dry laws (laws that forbid the sale of alcoholic beverages). In this era before antibiotics and other modern medical treatments, doctors often prescribed alcohol as a treatment for pain or anxiety. The WCTU pushed doctors to end this practice.

Besides fighting alcohol abuse, the WCTU advocated for better living conditions in prisons, an eight-hour workday for factory workers and other laborers, laws that restricted child labor, the founding of kindergartens, childcare for working mothers, facilities for neglected children, and job training for young women. A WCTU "social purity" program aimed at combating prostitution and sexually transmitted disease. The WCTU also advocated for world peace. The organization was successful in part because of its flexibility. It allowed local chapters to focus on whatever reforms they thought were most important.

The thing that tied all the reforms together, in Willard's mind, was the protection of the home and the family. Like the suffragists of the generation before her, Willard decided that all other reforms depended on one thing: women's votes.

Willard said that her decision to fight for suffrage came directly from God. She referred to woman suffrage as the "home protection ballot." She stressed that women would not leave behind their traditional roles as wives and mothers. They would bring those roles into the voting booth. She focused initially on winning woman suffrage in local and school board elections, in which women could vote for local dry laws and temperance education. But in 1883, the WCTU came out in favor of equal and unlimited suffrage for women. Willard argued that a woman belonged in politics, as she belonged everywhere, because she would have a cleansing effect on larger society. Willard liked to say, "Woman will bless and brighten every place she enters, and she will enter every place." This was a radical idea.

The WCTU's support for suffrage came when suffrage organizations were in decline. By the 1890s, the founders of the movement were old women and mostly retired. The two rival suffrage associations finally merged, and Anthony ran the new National American Woman Suffrage Association (NAWSA) for ten more years. But even she was slowing down, and the suffrage movement was not attracting new and younger supporters.

In contrast, the WCTU was growing. And while suffrage groups were mostly in the nation's largest cities, the WCTU flourished in smaller cities and towns. While suffragists were seen as radicals, temperance workers were more mainstream. The leading women of any community, including wives of ministers, professionals, and business owners, were all likely to join the WCTU. By 1895 the WCTU had 135,000 members, nearly ten times as many as NAWSA. Some suffrage organizations disbanded and their members joined the WCTU instead, continuing to fight for suffrage there. After Willard's death in 1898, the mission of the WCTU narrowed considerably. The new president focused almost exclusively on the fight to outlaw alcohol, but WCTU support for woman suffrage continued.

5

VOTES FOR WESTERN WOMEN

Wyoming Territory caught the nation by surprise in 1869. Late that year, territorial lawmakers voted to give the vote to white women, becoming the first territory in the United States to do so. The territory had not had a major suffrage campaign, nor did many white women even live in Wyoming. American Indian women lived there, but they were not citizens under territorial law. And the US Army was waging war against Indian nations in the West. Among Anglo-American settlers in Wyoming, men outnumbered women six to one.

How did this brand-new territory, populated by miners, ranchers, and railroad workers, become the first government to give women the vote? Part of the answer is that it was a brand-new government and a small one. Wyoming's first territorial congress, which convened in Cheyenne in 1869, consisted of an eight-member council and a twelve-member house. William H. Bright, a self-educated miner, saloonkeeper, and council president, was married to a suffragist. He and his fellow legislators were serious about women's rights. They passed a law guaranteeing equal pay for male and female teachers. They passed another law guaranteeing that married women could keep their property after divorce. Bright introduced the woman suffrage bill to the territorial government. It passed the council six votes to two. It moved on to the house, where it passed seven votes to four, with one member abstaining (declining to vote on the measure). The territorial governor signed the bill into law. The actions of

The first women's suffrage victories in the United States were in western states and territories. But the right to vote in the West did not extend to American Indian women, who were not legally US citizens at the time. This portrait of three generations of Ute women, taken by an unknown photographer, dates to the beginning of the twentieth century. The traditional homeland of the Ute Nation covered Utah, Colorado, Arizona, and New Mexico.

only fifteen men (counting the governor) were enough to make woman suffrage the law in Wyoming Territory.

Support for women's rights was not the lawmakers' only motivation. The Wyoming territorial congress first met during Reconstruction, shortly after the women's movement split over the Fifteenth Amendment. As Democrats, the Wyoming legislators were all strongly opposed to allowing black people to vote. Like many Americans, Bright believed that white women were superior to black men. In his mind, if black men had the vote, white women certainly should too. The law that passed in Wyoming gave the vote to white women only—not to women of color.

A desire for publicity also motivated the legislators. The suffrage debate was drawing more and more attention nationwide. Three other territories had narrowly defeated suffrage bills. If it became the first territory to pass woman suffrage, Wyoming was guaranteed a lot of press. Territorial leaders hoped this attention would attract more settlers, particularly women, to move to Wyoming. And with a larger population, the territory could apply for statehood. Wyoming Supreme Court judge John W. Kingman, a strong supporter of suffrage, wrote that among the arguments for the bill, "The favorite . . . and by far the most effective, was this: it would prove a great advertisement, would make a great deal of talk, and attract attention to the legislature, and the territory."

Wyoming's population did grow, and the territory petitioned to become a state in 1889. Some members of the US Congress objected to the woman suffrage section of the proposed state constitution. But Wyoming's women and men insisted that they would enter the union with woman suffrage or not at all. Congress and the US Senate voted for statehood. In 1890 Wyoming became a state, the first to allow women to vote.

COLORADO

When Colorado became a state in 1876, full woman suffrage was not included in its constitution. Colorado women were entitled to serve on school boards and to vote in school district elections, however. The constitution also specified that Colorado's first election after statehood would include a woman suffrage referendum (a question on the ballot for voters to pass into law or to reject). If more than 50 percent of voters supported it, the measure would pass.

In 1877 suffragists campaigned across the brand-new state. It wasn't easy. Coloradans were scattered among little Rocky Mountain mining towns hundreds of miles apart. Suffragist Margaret Campbell and her husband traveled more than 1,250 miles (2,012 km) in horse and buggy over steep mountain passes. Campbell cheerfully reported that woman suffrage was "the most prominent theme of public discussion" everywhere she went. "Miners discussed it around their campfires, and 'freighters' [people who transported supplies to the region by wagon] on their long slow journeys over the mountain trails argued pro and con whether they should 'let' women have the ballot."

Much of southern Colorado had until recently been part of Mexico, and many people in the state spoke Spanish. Suffragists tried to reach these voters through interpreters. They also held bilingual events with Spanish and English speakers.

ESTHER HOBART MORRIS: JUSTICE OF THE PEACE

A woman's right to vote in the West often came with other rights and responsibilities, such as the right to serve on juries and to hold public office. In 1870 Wyoming pioneer, entrepreneur, and suffragist Esther Hobart Morris (*left*) became the nation's first female justice of the peace (a judge who hears minor court cases).

Morris, who had little formal education, was nevertheless a competent justice. She kept firm control over her courtroom, telling quarreling lawyers, "Boys, behave yourselves." One of the lawyers who practiced before her reported that "to pettifoggers [unethical lawyers] she showed no mercy." During Morris's nine months in office, she decided twenty-six cases. And her record was good. Few of her rulings were appealed, and none of her rulings were reversed, or overturned by a higher court.

Though Campbell and other Colorado suffragists had a lot of enthusiasm, their suffrage organization was new and very small. The state's population was more than two-thirds male. Many of the women living in the state's mining towns were sex workers. The suffragists, who were generally married, did not feel comfortable recruiting sex workers to their cause.

Eastern suffragists came to Colorado to help. Susan B. Anthony, Lucy Stone, and Henry Blackwell all campaigned in Colorado. Audiences sometimes greeted the suffragists with enthusiastic applause, sometimes with hostility. Some Coloradans did not like women and men from the East coming into their state and telling them how to vote, and the referendum was soundly defeated, with 6,612 votes for and 14,053 against.

Colorado suffragists kept working. Veteran suffragists turned to the temperance issue to broaden their appeal. They helped found the Colorado WCTU in 1880. Mary Shields was president for its first five years. Drawing on Willard's arguments, she said that women had a duty to vote so that they could support laws to protect their homes and their families. She said their unique perspective as mothers, wives, and housekeepers gave them insights that would be useful for cleaning up government.

SECOND TRY

Like women in other cities, women in Denver—Colorado's capital city—formed literary clubs. They got together to discuss books, art, philosophy, and science. Before long, many women's clubs became interested in social reform. They began to raise money for good causes, such as kindergartens, playgrounds, and public libraries. They started to advocate for juvenile justice reform and child labor regulations. As they became more political, more and more of these clubs began to support woman suffrage.

A new referendum on woman suffrage in Colorado was planned for 1893. Carrie Chapman Catt, a rising star within the NAWSA, came to Colorado to help suffragists organize there. Until then the suffrage movement had gotten most of its support from middle-class women. Catt expanded her outreach by recruiting wealthy women with high social standing. Under her guidance, the suffragists won over several notable Denver socialites whose husbands had made fortunes in the silver-mining industry. Elizabeth "Baby Doe" Tabor convinced her husband, Horace "Silver King" Tabor, to donate money and office space to the suffragists. She and other socialites added status to the campaign. Journalist and suffrage organizer Minnie J. Reynolds bragged that "not one paper in Denver said a word of ridicule or even mild amusement concerning suffragists." She attributed this to the suffragists' success at winning over the city's "best people."

The suffragists also earned the backing of the People's Party—a party that had grown out of an alliance of farmers and laborers. To hold onto voters, the Democrats and Republicans in Colorado adopted some People's Party positions, including support for woman suffrage. No one bothered to organize much of an anti-suffrage campaign, and the woman suffrage referendum won by a comfortable 55 percent of the vote.

UTAH

Unlike other western territories, Utah had almost as many women as men by the mid-nineteenth century. Most of its white settlers were Mormons, members of the Church of Jesus Christ of Latter-day Saints. A controversial Mormon practice was plural marriage, or polygamy, in which leading men of the church took multiple wives. The US government and most non-Mormon Americans strongly opposed plural marriage. Most non-Mormons assumed that Mormon men forced women into plural marriages against their will. Eastern suffragists argued that Mormon women should have the vote so that they could free themselves. Congressional representative George W. Julian of Indiana thought that was a good idea. He introduced a bill that would have enfranchised Utah women. But it never went up for a vote.

Surprisingly, the woman suffrage idea appealed to Utah's political and religious leaders. The legislature of Utah Territory saw an opportunity to show the country that Mormon women were not oppressed. The Mormon Church, too, supported woman suffrage. Women voted in congregational elections, though they could not hold high offices in the church. So, on February 10, 1870, the Utah legislature unanimously voted to give women the vote. Just four days later, women voted for the first time in a municipal election in Salt Lake City.

Once the women of Utah were enfranchised, prominent women of the state worked to ensure that women would be informed voters. The Relief Society, a charitable women's organization linked to the Mormon Church, organized classes in government, history, and political science. Women became more active in public affairs. Some became lawyers, some served on school boards, and others served on juries.

To the disappointment of many non-Mormons, however, the women of Utah did not vote to end plural marriage. So in 1887, the US Congress passed the Edmunds-Tucker Act, which made plural marriage illegal and punishable by a fine or imprisonment. It also took away Utah women's right to vote. Men in Utah also could not vote, serve on juries, or be public officials unless they swore an oath against plural marriage. Because members of the Mormon Church refused to reject polygamy, this law disenfranchised all Mormons, men and women.

Finally, in 1890, the Mormon Church gave in to pressure from the federal government and officially ended its support for plural marriage. Then the US Congress gave Utah permission to apply for statehood. Susan B. Anthony congratulated the Woman's Suffrage Association of Utah. She was sure that after experiencing the sweetness of the vote and the bitterness of losing it, the women of Utah would make sure woman suffrage was included in their state constitution.

Utah suffragists convinced the Democratic and the Republican Parties to back woman suffrage in the new state constitution. Nevertheless, suffrage became the most contentious issue of the state constitutional convention. At the convention, some opponents worried that Utah voters or the US Congress would reject a state constitution that included woman suffrage. Non-Mormons in Utah worried that giving women the vote would further increase the Mormons' control over the government, since four out of five Utah women were Mormon. One delegate argued that politics was a dirty business and that "the refined wife and mother will not so much as put her foot in the filthy stream."

Another disagreed and called politics a "noble science," adding that women should not be confined to the job of "a wife, a mother, a cook, and a housekeeper."

Women suffrage won out. The Utah state constitution gave women the right to vote and hold public office. It guaranteed equal civil, political, and religious rights and privileges for male and female citizens. The US Congress approved the petition, and Utah became a state on January 4, 1896.

IDAHO, CALIFORNIA, AND OREGON

Support for suffrage in Idaho came from the same groups that had backed it in other western states: the People's Party, the temperance movement, and the Mormon population. In 1896 Idaho voters passed a woman suffrage referendum.

But after Idaho, several hard-fought suffrage campaigns on the West Coast ended in disappointment. In California and Oregon, the suffrage movement—with its strong ties to temperance—got pushback from brewers, distillers, and saloons. These businesses feared that if women got the right to vote, they would vote to

THE AWAKENING

This illustration from 1915 shows western states leading the way in women's suffrage. In the image, women in eastern and midwestern states are reaching for the suffrage torch carried by their western sister.

make liquor sales illegal. And the WCTU by then had successfully spearheaded many local and state bans on the manufacture and sale of alcohol. The group was even campaigning for a nationwide ban, which would become Prohibition.

Woman suffrage referenda in California and Oregon were defeated. Washington Territory enfranchised women in 1883, but the territorial supreme court overturned the law five years later. Between 1896 and 1910, a long period suffragists called the doldrums (a time of low spirits and inactivity), the woman suffrage movement had no victories.

6

NEW GENERALS, NEW TACTICS

By the beginning of the twentieth century, the woman suffrage movement had stalled. Its early leaders had died: Lucy Stone in 1893, Frances Willard in 1898, Elizabeth Cady Stanton in 1902, and Susan B. Anthony in 1906. The movement had lost direction and momentum.

Yet American women had made significant progress since the Seneca Falls Convention of 1848. By 1902, for example, three-quarters of states allowed married women to own property. States had established public school systems, and more girls than boys were getting a high school degree. Several prestigious private women's colleges were offering an elite education, and most public universities accepted women. More than one-third of college and university undergraduates were women.

Five million women were wage earners, and two-thirds of the states allowed married women to keep their own wages. In big cities, women worked in stores, offices, and factories. The 1870 US Census had listed only five female lawyers and notaries, or officers authorized by law to certify documents and do other legal tasks. By 1910 there were fifteen thousand. Over the same period, the number of female physicians and other health-care workers jumped from 550 to about 15,000. The number of women working as clergy and working for religious organizations and charities increased from sixty-seven to nearly ten thousand.

Families were changing as well. Divorce rates were rising. Nine states and the District of Columbia gave mothers and fathers shared custody of their children. And families were shrinking. The average woman had three or four children rather than seven or more.

Smaller families meant fewer demands on women's time. In the first decades of the twentieth century, power companies provided electricity to more and more American cities. With electricity in their homes, urban Americans purchased laborsaving electrical devices such as washing machines and vacuum cleaners. With these machines, women spent less time on housework. They had more leisure time, and many women joined social and civic clubs. About 100,000 women belonged to clubs in 1896. By 1914 this number had increased to 1 million. And the largest women's organization in the United States was the WCTU, with 245,000 members.

While the WCTU appealed to many American women, the suffrage movement had not kept up with the times. Anna Howard Shaw was the leader of NAWSA

In the early twentieth century, US cities grew rapidly and industry prospered. Many American women took jobs in urban factories and offices. By 1910 about five million US women held paying jobs. The women in this 1915 photo have clerical responsibilities in a US government office.

from 1904 to 1915. A bright, hardworking, highly motivated woman, Shaw had put herself through both theology school and medical school before becoming a WCTU lecturer. She was a gifted public speaker—forceful, humorous, witty, and quick thinking. For many years, she devoted herself to the suffrage cause, working as Susan B. Anthony's "bonnet holder"—a personal secretary and second-in-command. But Shaw was not an effective leader. She failed to make specific goals for the organization, to implement new recruiting methods, or to try new tactics. State and local branches were on their own, without any way to coordinate their efforts.

The suffrage movement was in a rut. According to Elizabeth Cady Stanton's daughter Harriot Stanton Blatch, "It bored its [supporters] and repelled its opponents." To make any headway, the movement needed new blood.

SELF-SUPPORTING WOMEN

For most of its history, the suffrage movement had appealed mostly to middle-class women. These women generally did not work outside the home. They spent their time raising families and volunteering for charities, churches, and reform organizations. Harriot Stanton Blatch saw that to be successful, the suffrage movement had to reach more women. So from 1907 to 1910, she made one of the largest efforts to reach employed women of all classes.

Blatch was Elizabeth Cady Stanton's second daughter and sixth child. At the age of twenty-six, she married English businessman William Henry Blatch Jr. She spent the next twenty years in England, where women were also fighting for suffrage. While her husband managed his family's brewery, she completed a study on working women's conditions in rural England, for which she earned a master's degree. She gave birth to two daughters, one of whom died at the age of four. And she was involved in several reform organizations, including the British suffrage movement. Blatch returned to the United States in 1902 to be with her dying mother and remained there for the rest of her life.

Unlike her mother, Blatch strongly opposed the idea of suffrage for educated people only. She believed that working-class people—black and white, men and women—needed the vote to improve their lives. During this era, many working-class Americans lived in cramped apartments, sometimes without heat or plumbing.

They often got sick from drinking unclean water and eating contaminated food. Few federal laws to protect health and safety existed. Those that did were poorly enforced, if at all. To scrape out a meager living, factory workers toiled long hours. They operated dangerous machinery, risking injury and even death. Women worked just as hard as men and for far less pay. Even children worked long hours in dangerous conditions to bring in extra money for their families. Blatch said that to ensure fair treatment by bosses and landlords, working Americans needed new laws. And to ensure those laws were passed, they needed the right to vote.

In 1907 Blatch started her own suffrage organization: the Equality League of Self-Supporting Women. She reached out to working women—from doctors to factory workers and from cooks to engineers. The league recruited entire labor unions, including two thousand female factory, laundry, and garment workers in New York City. These women worked in stuffy, poorly lit buildings for up to twelve hours a day, six or seven days a week. Many factory owners ignored regulations to protect workers' health and safety. Some bosses locked their workers into the factories, to prevent them from stealing or taking unauthorized breaks. Workers would have to get permission from a manager to use the restroom.

In November 1909, twenty thousand New York garment workers went on strike. They refused to go back to work until the factory owners agreed to increase their wages and provide safer working conditions. They set off a wave of strikes in other cities. These were the largest and longest strikes of female workers until then. Factory owners were furious. With no workers, production stopped, and the owners began to lose money. They called the police, who beat and arrested many of the strikers. Without wages, strikers struggled to feed their families.

The league and other women's organizations supported the striking workers. Middle-class and upper-class allies picketed with them, set up soup kitchens to feed strikers and their families, provided money for bail and lawyers, and acted as witnesses against abusive police and bosses. They hosted rallies to build public support for the strike. With this help, the strikers held out for more than two months. In February 1910, they settled with the factory owners for improved wages, better working conditions, and fewer hours.

Yet working conditions in many factories remained appalling. The Triangle Shirtwaist Factory took up the top three floors of a ten-story building in New York City. About 500 people worked there, most of them young immigrant women. On March 25, 1911, not long before quitting time, a fire started on the eighth floor. The building was not properly equipped with fire alarms, and many workers did not know about the fire until it was too late. Some of the exits were locked, and fire escapes were missing or broken. One fire escape collapsed in the heat of the fire, sending 20 people plunging to their deaths. More than 100 people were trapped inside the burning building. Firefighters' ladders did not reach beyond the sixth floor. So 62 people jumped or fell from the windows and were killed by the impact. Others remained inside the burning building and died from the flames or from smoke inhalation. In all, 146 died.

The Triangle Shirtwaist fire demonstrated how much working-class women needed the vote. They could not count on factory owners, city officials, or lawmakers to protect them. They needed to protect themselves, and they needed the ballot to do it.

A MILITANT EDUCATION

Alice Paul grew up in a tight-knit Quaker community in New Jersey. She was exceptionally bright and loved to study. After earning a bachelor's degree in biology from Swarthmore College in Pennsylvania, she went to London to study economics and social work. She wasn't satisfied with social work because she thought it made no real difference in her clients' lives. She found a more promising way to help society when she met the suffragettes.

In 1903 Emmeline Pankhurst and her daughter Christabel had founded the Women's Social and Political Union (WSPU) in Manchester, England. The group's motto was Deeds, Not Words. The WSPU believed that working politely for suffrage was not effective. British women needed to demand their rights. They needed to make a splash.

So the WSPU adopted militant methods. They took their cause out of private lecture halls and living rooms and into public spaces. Instead of speaking quietly inside, they stood on soapboxes and spoke on street corners. They organized large parades, rallies, and demonstrations. To draw attention to their cause, they even tried to be arrested. They slapped, charged at, or spit on the police. They threw rocks through the windows of government buildings. Critics tried to belittle the women by calling them suffragettes. (The suffix -ette, means "little female.") But the WSPU members loved the name and adopted it proudly. They used it to differentiate themselves from the more moderate British suffragists.

In England, Paul attended a lecture on suffrage at the University of Birmingham. Christabel Pankhurst was the main speaker. Paul was shocked to see male university students silence Pankhurst with boos and jeers. It immediately put her on the suffragettes' side. She attended a WSPU demonstration that attracted thousands of women and the event moved her. She loved the drama and excitement of the suffragettes' methods. Here at last were people willing to sacrifice their reputations, their safety, and even their liberty to make a difference in the world. Paul decided to join them. She spoke on street corners and gradually won the respect and trust of the Pankhursts. In June 1909, Emmeline Pankhurst invited her on an important mission. Pankhurst warned Paul that she should not go unless she was willing to be arrested. Paul accepted the challenge.

On June 29, she joined Pankhurst and other women in storming the British Parliament—where British lawmakers meet. The women asked to meet with Prime Minister Herbert Henry Asquith. After he refused to meet with them, the women threw themselves against police lines. The police grabbed them by the throats and threw them onto their backs. Planning for just such a response, they had worn layers of heavy winter clothes for padding.

Eventually, the police arrested the protesters and brought them to a police station. Among the battered suffragettes, Paul spotted a tall redhead sporting an American flag pin. Paul introduced herself. Lucy Burns was from Brooklyn, New York, the daughter of a well-off Irish Catholic banker. Like Paul, she had come to England to study and had been won over by the Pankhursts and the WSPU. She later wrote that she had started out skeptical, describing her introduction to the suffragettes this way: "I came to scoff, and remained to sell papers on the street . . . get carried off to jail, and eventually became an organizer for the Women's Social and Political Union in Edinburgh [Scotland]."

Emmeline Pankhurst (*center*) was a leading British suffragette. During an effort to deliver a suffrage petition to the king of England, George V, in May 1914, police arrested Pankhurst.

Paul and Burns planned and participated in many more attention-grabbing protests for the WSPU. Paul was arrested seven times and served three terms in jail. During her fourteen days in Holloway Prison in London in 1909, she and the other suffragettes refused to wear prison clothes. They wrapped themselves in blankets instead. They went on a hunger strike, refusing to eat until they were released. After five days without food, Paul was so weak that she was taken to the prison hospital on a stretcher. The doctor gave her a dose of brandy and sent her home.

Three months later, Paul, Burns, and another suffragette snuck into a banquet held in honor of the mayor of London. They broke a stained-glass window and shouted, "Votes for women!" For their disruption, they were sentenced to a month of hard labor at Holloway Prison. Meanwhile, the British government had found a way to deal with hunger strikers. Leaders knew they could not let the suffragettes starve to death. Not only would citizens view the government harshly, but they would also be more likely to view the suffragettes as martyrs. But the government did not want to release the protesters either, since they would go back to their illegal activities.

So the prisons put in place a new policy: force-feeding prisoners with liquids and soft food through tubes.

Force-feeding was brutal, painful, and humiliating. In late 1909, Paul described it to her mother and to the press. Three female prison wardens held her down, the largest one sitting astride her knees and holding her shoulders. One doctor forced her head back while another put a tube in her nostril. She wrote to her mother, "While the tube is going through the nasal passage it is exceedingly painful & only less so as it is being withdrawn. I never went through it without the tears streaming down my face." As she returned to her cell, blood was pouring from her nose.

Her nostrils swelled, and future feedings were even more painful. Paul fought the force-feeding each time. She told a London reporter, "Sometimes they tied me to a chair with sheets. Once I managed to get my hands loose and snatched the tube, tearing it with my teeth. I also broke a jug, but I didn't give in."

THE PARADE THAT BECAME A RIOT

In 1910, after two and a half years in England, Paul returned to the United States. Burns returned two years later. Determined to revitalize the American woman suffrage movement, Paul wrangled a position as head of the NAWSA's Congressional Union for Woman Suffrage in 1912. This much-neglected department was supposed to lobby (try to influence) members of Congress, but it had done little in recent years. With an annual budget of only thirteen dollars and little support from the main organization, not much was expected of the Congressional Union for Woman Suffrage. But Paul had big plans.

She had decided that the state-by-state approach to winning suffrage was taking too long. What suffragists needed was a constitutional amendment enfranchising all the women of the country. She needed to draw as much attention as possible to the idea. She decided to stage a parade. She would hold it in Washington, DC, the day before the inauguration of the newly elected president, Woodrow Wilson. The city would be filled with people, including reporters.

Paul and a team of volunteers spent months raising money, negotiating with the city for permits and police protection, ordering costumes and banners, and coordinating construction of a fleet of floats. Women from all over the country

Suffragists on foot and horseback parade down Pennsylvania Avenue in Washington, DC, in March 1913. Shortly after the parade began, angry crowds of men assailed them—pushing, jeering, and even spitting on them.

responded enthusiastically to the call for marchers. When black women asked to join the parade, it raised a dilemma for Paul. She did not want to turn them away. But she did not want to offend white women from the South, where racism was harshest. Paul feared that southern women would drop out of the parade if black women joined in. After much hesitation and deliberation, Paul and the other organizers agreed that black women could participate but only a few and at the end of the procession.

On the day of the parade, March 3, 1913, somewhere between five and eight thousand women lined up, ready to march down Pennsylvania Avenue. At the head of the parade was prominent suffragette Inez Milholland on a white horse. Close behind came a wagon emblazoned with the words, "WE DEMAND AN AMENDMENT TO THE CONSTITUTION OF THE UNITED STATES ENFRANCHISING THE WOMEN OF THIS COUNTRY." Renowned journalist and black rights activist Ida Wells-Barnett was offended and hurt when organizers told her she would have to move to the "Negro" section of the parade. The Chicago resident insisted that she would march under the Illinois banner or not at all. Two white women supported her, but the organizers

THE SUFFRAGETTES SUCCEED

After Paul and Burns returned to the United States, the British suffragettes continued their campaign, with ever more dramatic and violent protests. Suffragettes cut telephone wires, poured ink and acid into mailboxes, and set fires at empty golf courses, cricket grounds, and horse racing tracks. They set off bombs, damaging a house being built for a government official, and attacked a portrait of the Duke of Wellington in the National Gallery with an ax.

These destructive acts deeply divided the movement, and they mostly ended in 1914, with the start of World War I. The WSPU stopped its militant acts and supported the war.

On February 6, 1918, the British Parliament passed the Representation of the People Act, which gave all men over twenty-one the right to vote. (Previously, men had needed to meet property ownership requirements to vote.) The act also gave women over the age of thirty—who met certain property requirements—the right to vote. The British government explained the age difference by noting that because so many young men had been killed in World War I, women voters would have outnumbered men if all women over twenty-one were allowed to vote—and the government did not trust women to make up a majority of the electorate. In 1928 the British government changed the law so that women could start voting at the age of twenty-one.

held firm. Wells-Barnett left the lineup temporarily, but rejoined the Illinois delegation once the march was under way.

As soon as the parade began, male spectators swarmed past the barriers protecting the parade route. The men, many of them drunk, taunted the women, and some physically attacked them. One man slapped Nora Blatch de Forest, daughter of Harriot Stanton Blatch and granddaughter of Elizabeth Cady Stanton, in the face hard enough to leave a mark. Another spat chewing tobacco juice into the face of an elderly woman.

The marchers fought their way slowly down the street while police looked on without helping. With the situation completely out of control, the police superintendent sent for cavalry troops from nearby Fort Myer. The horse-mounted soldiers charged into the crowds to clear the avenue. The marchers traveled the last few blocks of their route in peace.

Paul's plan of attracting attention had succeeded beyond her wildest imaginings. People who read about the debacle in the newspaper were horrified at how the suffragists had been treated and outraged at the police's failure to protect them. Paul wrote to a supporter, "This mistreatment by the police was probably the best thing that could ever have happened to us as it aroused a great deal of public indignation and sympathy."

A SUFFRAGE MARTYR

From the beginning, Alice Paul clashed with NAWSA president Anna Howard Shaw, who rightly saw Paul as a threat to her authority. In 1914 Paul withdrew from NAWSA, taking Lucy Burns and her other supporters with her. She started her own organization, which after several mergers and name changes became the National Woman's Party.

Alice Stone Blackwell, daughter of Lucy Stone and Henry Blackwell, disapproved of Paul's radical tendencies and blamed her for once again splitting the movement. But Harriot Stanton Blatch and Paul were natural allies. After a New York state suffrage referendum failed in 1916, Blatch and her colleagues merged their organization with Paul's and focused on the campaign for a federal amendment.

Following the example of the British suffragettes, Blatch and Paul decided to hold the party in power responsible for the lack of progress on suffrage. This meant targeting the Democrats, with Woodrow Wilson as president, a majority in the US Senate, and a two-thirds majority in the House of Representatives. The state-by-state approach to suffrage had continued, and by 1916, women could vote in twelve states. This meant that more than 3.5 million women could vote in presidential elections. The National Woman's Party went to those states and campaigned against all Democrats, even those who supported suffrage. They hoped that the threat of losing women's votes would pressure the Democrats into passing a suffrage amendment.

Harriot Stanton Blatch spearheaded the campaign. Another of the campaign's most popular speakers was Inez Milholland. She had been arrested for picketing with striking shirtwaist workers in New York City before becoming a labor lawyer. She had also spent time as a war correspondent in Italy in 1915, before the United States entered World War I (1914–1918).

Paul set a demanding schedule for the 1916 campaign: fifty meetings in twelve states over thirty days. By the time Milholland reached Chicago, her first destination, she felt sick. She was dizzy and achy, and her heart was skipping beats. A doctor recommended immediate removal of her tonsils. Not wanting to let down the National Woman's Party, Milholland asked for medication instead and continued the tour. Despite her illness, Milholland gave inspiring speeches. For nineteen days, she won over converts and brought in donations. Then, in Los Angles, she collapsed in the middle of an impassioned speech. She was helped from the stage. Fifteen minutes later, she was back. Her colleague Beulah Amidon reported, "Miss Milholland was thrilling and they were thrilled."

Milholland's condition was much more serious than Amidon thought. As soon as the event concluded, Milholland was hospitalized. Doctors diagnosed her with pernicious anemia. They judged her too weak to survive an operation to remove her infected tonsils and several infected teeth. Her condition continued to worsen. On November 25, 1916, she died. Her last public words were, "Mr. President, how long must women wait for liberty?"

On Christmas Day, the National Woman's Party held an elaborate and emotional memorial for Milholland in the Capitol's National Statuary Hall. Many congressional representatives and senators had been honored there. This was the first memorial for a woman held there. Posters read, "Inez Milholland Boissevain [her married name], Who Died for the Freedom of Women" and showed her astride her white horse, carrying a banner bearing the motto Forward into Light. This image became the official logo of the National Woman's Party.

7

WAR ON TWO FRONTS

Even with new strategies, the women's suffrage campaign had not been successful in passing a national suffrage amendment. Something more had to be done. The National Woman's Party decided to picket the White House. Blatch implored her supporters: "Won't you come and join us in standing day after day at the gates of the White House with banners asking, 'What will you do, Mr. President, for one-half the people of this nation?' Stand there as sentinels [guards]—sentinels of liberty, sentinels of self-government, silent sentinels."

At the time, this idea was shocking. No one had ever picketed the White House before. Many suffragists thought it was unladylike, undignified, and disrespectful. Members quit the organization in protest and canceled their subscriptions to the *Suffragist* newspaper. Even Paul's mother asked her to call it off. But some suffragists loved the idea. Alva Belmont, an extremely rich New York suffragist, sent the National Woman's Party a $5,000 check, the equivalent of about $100,000 in twenty-first-century dollars.

From January 10 to March 4, 1917, the "silent sentinels" stood in the cold, wet, miserable winter weather at the White House gates every day except Sunday. They held gold, white, and purple banners and held signs that said, "HOW LONG MUST WOMEN WAIT FOR LIBERTY?" The president politely tipped his hat as he went by and had the White House guards invite them inside for coffee. Since the invitation

As president of the National American Woman Suffrage Association, Carrie Chapman Catt organized suffragists at the state and national levels. An opponent of picketing and demonstrations, Catt preferred to make change through nonconfrontational political efforts.

did not include a meeting with the president, they declined.

Tourists sometimes laughed, jeered, or tried to argue with them. But other passersby offered encouragement and sympathy. Women brought them hot bricks to warm the bottoms of their feet, thermoses of coffee, mittens, fur pieces, galoshes, and raincoats. An old Civil War veteran told the sentinels, "You gotta fight for your rights in this world, and now that we are about to plunge into another war, I want to tell you women there'll be no end to it unless you women get power."

A "WINNING PLAN"

In 1915 Carrie Chapman Catt, who had helped organize the winning Colorado campaign, became president of NAWSA. Valuing harmony, cooperation, and diplomacy over all, she tried unsuccessfully to reconcile with Paul. While she hoped to keep the movement together, she did not support Paul's methods. She thought campaigning against the entire Democratic Party was foolish and counterproductive. It would only alienate Democratic allies. And she particularly hated the picketing. It went against everything she thought politics should be. Catt was an ardent pacifist (one who objects to war) and thought that Paul's tactics were too warlike. Rather than trying to annoy or embarrass the president, she preferred to try to win him over with friendliness and pleasantness.

When she could not convince the National Woman's Party to give up its militant methods, Catt publicly rejected the group. She spread the word through newspaper interviews that NAWSA was not involved in the picketing and did not support it. Since NAWSA had two million members—and the National Woman's Party only fifty thousand—she could rightly claim to represent most suffragists.

But Catt did agree with Paul that it was time to get a federal suffrage amendment passed. She knew this would be a massive undertaking and would require extensive support from the states. Thirty-six of the nation's forty-eight states would have to vote to approve the amendment. Catt was determined to set up support at the state level by the time the amendment got through Congress.

Catt was an excellent organizer and savvy strategist. She quietly organized her extensive army of supporters into a coordinated plan of attack. In August 1916, she gave each state an assignment. NAWSA chapters in the suffrage states, where women already had the right to vote, were to convince their state legislatures to ask Congress to pass a suffrage amendment. Chapters in states such as New York, where suffrage seemed promising, were to continue to campaign for state suffrage amendments. Other eastern and northern states, where suffrage support was moderately high, should try to win suffrage for women in presidential elections. State legislatures could usually pass this law without voter approval. It would be easier than getting suffrage for all elections. NAWSA chapters in southern states, where support for suffrage still lagged, should try to get the right to vote in primary elections. By voting in primary elections, women would help select the candidates that parties chose to run in state and federal elections.

TURNING UP THE HEAT

Meanwhile, war was threatening. Europe had been consumed by World War I since July 1914. The Allies, led by Britain, France, and Russia, fought battle after bloody battle against the Central powers, led by Germany and Austria-Hungary. Many Americans feared that the United States would be pulled into the conflict. German submarines had begun to sink US ships transporting goods to Europe. More and more people called for the United States to enter the war on the side of the Allies.

Many suffragists, including Catt and Paul, were pacifists. But Catt recognized that trying to stop the United States from entering the war was "like throwing a violet at a stone wall." Thinking strategically, she decided to support the war effort and to throw NAWSA's support behind it as well. The United States did eventually enter the war, on April 7, 1917. NAWSA encouraged suffragists to get involved by working for international aid organizations such as the Red Cross. Catt herself served on the Women's Committee of the Council of National Defense. And she made sure to publicize the patriotism of the NAWSA and its members.

While Catt demonstrated the patriotism and good citizenship of women, Paul used the war differently. When French and English diplomats visited the White House, the silent sentinels were there at the gates. They carried banners bearing Wilson's own words in support of US involvement in the war: "We shall fight for the things we have always held nearest to our hearts." They emphasized the irony of fighting for democracy abroad while the US excluded half of its population from democracy. "Democracy should begin at home," their banners said.

In June 1917, a diplomatic delegation from Russia visited the White House. As the delegation approached the White House gates in cars, Burns and another suffragist held up a banner. It read, "To the Russian envoys, we the women of America tell you that America is not a democracy, twenty million American women are denied the right to vote. President Wilson is the chief opponent to their national enfranchisement. Help us make this nation really free. Tell our government it must liberate its people before it can claim free Russia as an ally."

The banner infuriated a crowd of spectators, who ripped it down and destroyed it. The next day, the press condemned the National Woman's Party as traitors to their country and accused them of damaging the war effort. Paul replied, "The intolerable conditions against which we protest can be changed in a twinkling of an eye. The responsibility for our protest is, therefore, with the Administration and not with the women of America, if the lack of democracy at home weakens the Administration in its fight for democracy three thousand miles [4,828 km] away."

BEHIND BARS

The government warned the National Woman's Party that it must stop picketing or its members would be arrested. It did not stop. Over the next few days, silent sentinels were arrested and falsely charged with obstructing traffic.

JEANNETTE RANKIN: SUFFRAGIST, PACIFIST, CONGRESSWOMAN

Montana voters elected Jeannette Pickering Rankin (*leaning over the balcony*) to the US Congress in 1916, four years before many American women could vote. A social worker and dedicated suffragist, she had helped make Montana a suffrage state in 1914. She ran for Congress on a platform of equal suffrage, Prohibition, and child welfare.

Rankin was a committed pacifist. Only three days after being sworn into office, she voted against the United States entering World War I. Rankin said, "I want to stand by my country, but I cannot vote for war."

While in office, she worked hard to get the Susan B. Anthony Amendment through the House of Representatives. In January 1918, she opened the first House floor debate on the topic, saying, "How shall we answer [women's] challenge gentlemen? How shall we explain to them the meaning of democracy if the same Congress that voted for war to make the world safe for democracy refuses to give this small measure of democracy to the women of our country?"

In 1918 Rankin ran for the US Senate and lost. She went on to spend two decades working for peace and social reform. She returned to Congress in the fall of 1941, just before Japan attacked a US naval base at Pearl Harbor. She cast her vote on whether the United States should enter World War II (1939–1945), holding firm to her pacifist principles. She said, "As a woman I cannot go to war, and I refuse to send anyone else." She was the only member of Congress to vote against the war resolution.

The first six picketers to go to trial had their day in court on June 26, 1917. The judge found them guilty, scolded them for their "unpatriotic, almost treasonable behavior," and sentenced them to a twenty-five-dollar fine or three days in jail. They refused to pay the fine and went to jail.

The suffragists continued to picket. With more arrests every day, the judge decided he would have to be stricter. He sentenced a group of suffragists to sixty days in Occoquan Workhouse, a prison in Virginia. Conditions in the workhouse were wretched. The women received blankets that were washed only once a year. They were denied toothbrushes, combs, handkerchiefs, and soap. The food—beans, hominy, rice, cornmeal, and cereal—was infested with worms. To amuse themselves, the suffragists counted the worms, collected them in a spoon, and sent them to the prison's superintendent.

Wilson pardoned the suffragists after they had spent three days in the workhouse. If Wilson hoped this would cool the campaign of the National Woman's Party, he was disappointed. Rather than backing down, the women stepped up their attacks on the president. On August 14, the sentinels displayed a banner addressing Wilson as Kaiser Wilson. By using the title for the German leader, they were comparing the president to the enemy. Crowds around the White House were outraged. Off-duty army soldiers and navy sailors attacked the suffragists. They snatched the banner and destroyed it. Then they chased the protesters down the street. The sentinels retreated to the party's headquarters, where they hung their remaining banners from the second-floor balcony. Three sailors climbed the outside of the building, tore down the banners and the US flag, and punched a young woman in the face. Police did nothing until someone fired a shot through a second-floor window. Then the police finally broke up the mob. The men who had attacked the women were not arrested.

The following days brought further confrontations between the sentinels and hostile crowds. The police joined the mob in ripping off the women's sashes and destroying their banners. They then arrested the suffragists, letting their attackers go free. This time, the judge sentenced the suffragists to thirty to sixty days in Washington Jail. Because the jail didn't have room for all of them, many of them were sent to the Occoquan Workhouse instead.

In both Washington Jail and the Occoquan Workhouse, the sentinels demanded to be treated as political prisoners. They argued that they had not committed any crime but had been imprisoned for their political beliefs. They refused to wear prison clothes, to work, or to cooperate with prison officials in any way.

Officials put Lucy Burns in solitary confinement, hoping that would stop the rebellion. But the suffragists began a hunger strike, passing notes to one another through holes in the walls to coordinate their efforts. They smuggled some of these notes out of jail to let their sympathizers know what was going on, including force-feeding.

Meanwhile, the National Woman's Party continued to picket and the police continued to arrest suffragists. In October, Paul received a seven-month sentence in Washington Jail. She immediately set out to be as uncooperative as possible, throwing a smuggled book through a window to let in some fresh air. A psychiatrist came to evaluate her. He invited her to talk about suffrage and she did, remaining calm and composed as she lectured at length on her favorite topic. Officials had her committed to the psychiatric ward. She refused to eat and was force-fed. The suffragist in the next cell heard her screams during the feedings.

On November 23, 1917, the Occoquan Workhouse suffrage prisoners went to court. Their condition shocked the public. Some of them had to lie on the benches because they were too weak to sit up straight. With mounting pressure from the public and a strain on prison resources, officials relented. All suffrage prisoners were released on

Lucy Burns spent more time in jail than any other suffragist. Arrested numerous times in both Britain and the United States, she endured force-feeding and solitary confinement. Here she sits in Occoquan Workhouse in Washington, DC, in 1917.

November 27 and 28. The National Woman's Party honored them with a ceremony. Each former prisoner—ninety-seven in all—received a small silver pin shaped like a prison door with a heart-shaped lock. On the lock were the words, "a badge of courage for those who had been jailed for freedom."

FINAL BATTLES

Woman suffrage had friends in the House of Representatives. One of them was Jeannette Rankin, a Republican from Montana. She was the first—and the only—woman in Congress. As the suffragists picketed and suffered behind bars, Rankin and other pro-suffrage legislators pushed their colleagues to consider the Susan B. Anthony Amendment. On January 10, 1918, exactly one year after the silent sentinels first stationed themselves in front of the White House gates, the amendment came up for a vote in the House of Representatives.

Rankin started the proceedings with a speech in favor of the bill. To pass it in the House, supporters needed 274 votes to achieve the required two-thirds majority. Several suffrage supporters made heroic efforts to be present for the vote. One congressional representative arrived on a stretcher straight from an appendectomy. Another refused to have a broken shoulder set before he gave his vote, and a third returned from a six-month hospital stay in Baltimore to vote. Frederick Hicks Jr. of New York showed up to honor his suffragist wife, who had died the night before. The suffragists got exactly the number of votes they needed, with 274 for and 136 against. Paul did not take time to celebrate. Before the vote was even final, she was back at work, strategizing about the vote in the Senate. The suffragists still had eleven more senators to persuade.

Lobbyists with the National Woman's Party and NAWSA spent months talking to reluctant senators, bargaining, and campaigning. Meanwhile, the National Woman's Party also started a new round of demonstrations in Lafayette Park, just north of the White House. The police arrested each woman who stepped forward to speak. This time, the suffragists were charged with holding a public meeting without a permit and "climbing a statue."

By then Congress had vowed it would pass only legislation directly related to the war, so suffragists wanted the president to ask the Senate to pass the suffrage amendment as a war measure—using the argument that giving women the vote would demonstrate to the world the US commitment to democracy. While Catt applied pressure privately and diplomatically, the National Woman's Party returned to Lafayette Park for more protests.

Finally, the day before the Senate vote, Wilson obliged. He appeared before the Senate and declared that passage of the suffrage amendment was "vitally essential to the successful prosecution" of the war. The president's last-minute entreaty did no good. The amendment lost in the Senate by two votes. Carrie Chapman Catt was furious. Breaking her commitment to political neutrality, she told NAWSA to campaign against legislators who had voted against suffrage.

The National Woman's Party was also outraged. It moved its protests away from the president and directed them at the Senate. Picketing the Capitol, members held banners that accused the Senate of obstructing the war effort and siding with the enemy by denying self-government to the people.

Just over a month later, on November 11, 1918, World War I ended. The Allies had won. Wilson turned to peace negotiations. He wanted to build an international association of nations to prevent future wars. The last thing he needed was the bad publicity of a public fight over enfranchisement at home—especially when many nations in Europe had already granted women the vote.

Under pressure from the suffragists and pro-suffrage senators, the Senate majority leader scheduled another vote on the suffrage amendment. It failed again but by only one vote.

In the congressional elections of 1918, Republicans gained a majority in both the House of Representatives and the Senate. Many of the newly elected legislators were more open to suffrage than their predecessors had been. On May 21, 1919, the Susan B. Anthony Amendment easily passed in the House of Representatives. The vote was 304 to 89—42 votes more than needed. Two weeks later, the Senate vote was narrower but decisive, 56 to 25. The fight moved to the states.

NAWSA leaders wrote to governors, begging them, "in honor of our Nation, in respect to the history which is now being made in the world around, to see that [your state] makes its contribution of ratification in such time that posterity will not blush at the hesitancy of our country to put this amendment into the

Alice Paul raises a toast to celebrate ratification of the Nineteenth Amendment in 1920.

Constitution." Several states raced to be the first to ratify the woman suffrage amendment. Wisconsin came first, six days after the amendment had passed the Senate. Illinois and Michigan followed closely behind. By the end of May, Kansas, Ohio, New York, Pennsylvania, Massachusetts, and Texas had ratified it.

Other states were more reluctant. The Eighteenth Amendment—banning the production, importation, transportation, and sale of alcoholic beverages—had gone into effect on January 16, 1920. Prohibition was the law of the land. The liquor industry feared that if women got the vote, Prohibition would never be repealed. They threatened to kill the careers of any governors or state lawmakers who helped ratify the Nineteenth Amendment.

After a year of campaigning, thirty-five states had ratified the amendment. Only one more was needed, and Tennessee looked like the suffragists' best hope. It came down to twenty-four-year-old Harry Burn, the youngest member of the Tennessee House of Representatives. Burn came from a conservative district. Few of the people in his district supported suffrage. But tucked into his pocket was a letter from his mother. It read, "Vote for suffrage. . . . Don't forget to be a good boy and help Mrs. Catt put 'Rat' in Ratification." (This last sentence of the letter referred to a political cartoon showing a woman chasing the letters *r*, *a*, and *t* with a broom, trying to complete the word *ratification*.)

Uncertain until the last minute, Burn ultimately decided "that a mother's advice is always safest for her boy to follow," and he cast the deciding vote for suffrage. Two days later, on August 26, 1920, the US secretary of state, Robert Lansing, signed off on the Nineteenth Amendment, making it officially part of the US Constitution. Millions of women would vote for the first time in elections that November.

WHO GOT THERE FIRST? WOMAN SUFFRAGE AROUND THE WORLD

The first nation to enfranchise all women was New Zealand, which did so in 1893. Women in New Zealand were not allowed to run for office until 1919. Australia enfranchised women in 1902. However, Aboriginal (indigenous Australian) women and men were excluded from voting until 1962. In 1906 Finland became the first nation to allow women to both vote and run for office.

More than twenty nations granted women suffrage in the 1910s. They included many European nations. Canada granted women the vote in 1918, but Canada's First Nations (indigenous) women could not vote until 1960. Throughout the rest of the twentieth century, more than one hundred more nations, including the United States in 1920, granted women the right to vote.

As late as the twenty-first century, some women still didn't have the right to vote. Women in Kuwait and Iraq finally got the vote in 2005. Women in the United Arab Emirates got the right to vote in 2006, and women in Saudi Arabia got it in 2011. The only country that does not allow women to vote is Vatican City, the smallest nation on Earth (with only about one thousand citizens) and headquarters of the Roman Catholic Church.

8

UNFINISHED BUSINESS

In 1920 pollsters did not ask people whether they voted, so historians do not know how many women voted in the first presidential election after passage of the Nineteenth Amendment. Researchers do know that voters cast about eight million more votes than in the previous presidential election, so probably women cast most of them.

Turnout varied widely by region. In New York City, women often outnumbered men at the polls. In New Jersey, turnout was so high that the ballot boxes overflowed and had to be replaced by barrels. Throughout the South, black women were turned away from the polls, and many southern white women chose not to vote.

In Washington, DC, Paul voted by absentee ballot rather than go home to vote in Moorestown, New Jersey. Her mother, Tacie Paul, wrote in her diary, "During the Summer suffrage was granted to women & we voted for the first time for President Nov. 1920. Alice at last saw her dream realized."

Passing the Nineteenth Amendment doubled the pool of eligible voters in the United States, and politicians were eager to capture their votes. To appeal to women, many politicians in the 1920s emphasized their support for Prohibition, health and safety regulations, public schools, and world peace. But it soon became clear that women did not all share the same opinions or vote as a block for the same candidates. Politicians saw that people's votes were often influenced more by their social class, race, ethnic group, and religion than by their gender.

The League of Women Voters formed in February 1920, about six months before passage of the Nineteenth Amendment. Before the 1920 presidential election, the league presented a list of concerns to the Democratic Party. Issues included child welfare, education, food costs, women's employment, and public health. By promising to address these issues, candidates had a better chance of winning the support of newly enfranchised female voters.,

Nevertheless, the 1920s did see some important political accomplishments for American women. They successfully lobbied lawmakers for programs such as the Sheppard-Towner Act of 1921. This act provided money for health care and education for pregnant women, new mothers, and infants. And the Cable Act of 1922 allowed American women married to foreigners to keep their US citizenship. Before then women who married someone from another country automatically lost their US citizenship. Legislators passed these laws to win over women voters. But by the end of the 1920s, politicians were already taking women's votes for granted. The Sheppard-Towner Act lapsed in 1929, and lawmakers didn't renew it.

NO VOTES FOR BLACK WOMEN—OR BLACK MEN

The Fifteenth Amendment forbids racial discrimination in voting. Yet many states and counties found ways to get around the law. Poll taxes and literacy tests remained in many parts of the South. These barriers kept the ballot away from black women as well as black men.

Jim Crow laws also continued segregation, especially in the South. And because black Americans were kept from good-paying jobs, most black communities were poor. Nationwide, most banks would not lend money to black Americans to start businesses. Schools for black children were substandard, and many colleges would not accept black students. Many black families remained poor for generations. Many black voters could not afford to pay poll taxes.

Literacy tests were not designed to ensure that only people who could read and write could vote but to ensure that only *white* people could vote. Different states had different tests, but they often required potential voters to read aloud a portion of the state or federal constitution and explain what it meant. Officials gave white voters easy and straightforward passages. They gave black voters highly technical sections, which only a legal scholar would understand. Election officials determined which answers passed and which failed. Sometimes whites were allowed to skip the literacy tests altogether. Blacks never were.

"THE FREEDOM BANNER"

Starting in the 1950s, civil rights activists risked their lives to fight against Jim Crow segregation. Using nonviolent protest, they drew attention to the racial injustices in the United States. In Montgomery, Alabama, city laws required black riders to sit in the backs of buses and to give up their seats to whites. To protest the law, black citizens launched a bus boycott. They refused to ride buses until the city changed its policies. Without black customers, the city bus program lost money. After the boycott continued for more than a year, the city finally dropped the discriminatory laws. Civil rights activists also organized peaceful sit-ins at restaurants that refused to serve black customers. They organized swim-ins at pools that refused to allow black swimmers. And they started registration drives to register black voters. All sorts of people, both black and white, participated in the protests. Police retaliation against them was often brutal. Police officers sometimes set vicious dogs on protesters or sprayed them with tear gas or water from high-pressure fire hoses.

In 1962 Fannie Lou Hamer and seventeen other black citizens decided to go together to register to vote in Indianola, Mississippi. The clerk turned away most of them immediately. Only Hamer and one other applicant were allowed to begin to register. The clerk wrote down their names, addresses, and employers and gave them the required literacy test. Hamer, who had worked in cotton fields alongside her parents and siblings since she was six years old, had little formal education. But she could read and write. The clerk asked her to explain a portion of the state constitution about de facto laws (regulations that are in place without legal authorization). Hamer said later that she knew "as much about a facto law as a horse knows about Christmas day." She failed the test. And Hamer lost her job. Her white boss fired her for trying to register to vote.

Hamer was committed to gaining the vote for herself and other African Americans. "I guess if I'd had any sense, I'd a been a little scared," she said later. "But what was the point of being scared? The only thing the whites could do was kill me, and it seemed like they'd been trying to do that a little bit at a time since I could remember." In June 1963, Hamer attended a voter registration workshop with other civil rights activists in South Carolina. On the way home, their bus stopped at a rest stop. Five of the black activists tried to eat at a segregated restaurant there. Police arrested everyone on the bus, including Hamer, who hadn't even gone into the restaurant. They took her to jail, where they called her ugly names. She could hear the police beating and threatening other civil rights activists nearby. Then they came into her cell. They made her lie on a bed and forced two male African American prisoners to take turns beating her with a blackjack (a heavy leather pouch filled with lead). The beating caused a limp and other health problems for the rest of her life.

After her release, Hamer led the push to register black voters in her home state of Mississippi. Mississippi's Democratic Party did not allow blacks to join the party. So Hamer and two other civil rights activists cofounded the integrated Mississippi Freedom Democratic Party. Hamer ran unsuccessfully for Congress as a Mississippi Freedom Democrat in 1964. That year she also traveled to Ohio, where she visited churches and trained volunteers to register voters. A journalist described one of her efforts to encourage church parishioners to vote: "Mrs. Hamer rose majestically to her feet. Her magnificent voice rolled through the chapel as she enlisted the

Fannie Lou Hamer asks to have Mississippi Freedom Democratic Party delegates seated at the 1964 Democratic National Convention in Atlantic City, New Jersey. DNC leaders refused to seat those delegates, but they did allow Hamer to address a convention committee. At that meeting, she talked about the mistreatment and discrimination she endured as a black American and civil rights activist.

Biblical ranks of martyrs and heroes to summon these folk to the Freedom banner. Her mounting, rolling battery of quotations and allusions from the Old and New Testaments stunned the audience with its thunder."

BLOODY SUNDAY

By the mid-1960s, the civil rights movement had become a visible political force. Under intense pressure from American voters and from civil rights leaders such as Martin Luther King Jr., President Lyndon B. Johnson eventually persuaded the US Congress to pass the Civil Rights Act of 1964. This landmark legislation bans racial segregation in schools, places of work, and public establishments such as restaurants and hotels. The act also bans discrimination based on religion, national origin, and sex.

Even with the new law, southern leaders were determined to prevent black people from voting. After a state trooper shot and killed voting rights activist Jimmie Lee Jackson during a peaceful march in Alabama in 1965, Martin Luther King Jr. and other civil rights leaders planned a voting rights march. The route would go from Selma, Alabama, to the state capital of Montgomery, about 50 miles (80 km) away.

On March 7, 1965, later known as Bloody Sunday, six hundred women and men lined up to march for their voting rights. The protesters made it only six blocks, to the Edmund Pettus Bridge. At the bridge, they were met by dozens of blue-helmeted Alabama state troopers and a sheriff's posse of dozens more men, some on horseback. Crowds of white spectators shouted and waved Confederate flags—a symbol of white supremacy. The law enforcement officers attacked the protesters with tear gas, trampled them with horses, and beat them with clubs the size of baseball bats.

The violence horrified the nation. Two days later, on March 9, protesters marched again and police officers confronted them. White segregationists armed with clubs beat white minister and civil rights activist James Reeb to death. Horrified, Johnson gave a speech on national television the next week. He promised to support the Selma marchers and to pass voting rights legislation. He told the American people, "There is no Negro problem. There is no Southern problem. There is no Northern problem. There is only an American problem." He went on to say, "Their cause must be our cause too. Because it is not just Negroes, but really it is all of us, who must overcome the crippling legacy of bigotry and injustice. And we *shall* overcome."

Johnson convinced Congress to pass the Voting Rights Act of 1965, and he signed it into law on August 6. The act outlawed poll taxes and literacy tests. It prohibited state and local governments from imposing any voting law that discriminated against any racial or language minority group. It also required certain state and local governments to get federal approval before changing their voting regulations.

On August 14, 1965, just eight days after Johnson signed the act into law, the US Justice Department sent federal voting examiners to Selma to register black voters. They registered 381 black voters in a single day, more than Dallas County (in which Selma is located) had registered over the previous sixty-five years. By November the county had 8,000 new black voters. They used their hard-won power to vote Sheriff Jim Clark, who had led the Bloody Sunday attack against the marchers, out of office.

On the Edmund Pettus Bridge in Selma, Alabama, police violently attacked civil rights marchers on March 7, 1965. Amelia Boynton (*center, held up by two fellow marchers*) was beaten unconscious.

It had taken more than forty years after the passage of the Nineteenth Amendment for the promise of equal suffrage to become a reality for black women. And once they and black men were able to vote, their impact was real. Black voters helped elect seventy-two black officials in the South in 1965 and many more in the following years and decades. Some of these officials were women. In 1968, for example, Shirley Chisholm became the first black woman in Congress, representing New York's Twelfth District. She served seven terms in Congress and made an unsuccessful yet prominent bid for president in 1972.

WOMEN RISE AGAIN

As abolition had done more than a century before, the struggle for civil rights helped trigger another social justice movement—the renewed struggle for women's rights. Besides participating in the civil rights movement, many young people of the 1960s protested US involvement in the Vietnam War (1957–1975). Women of all backgrounds, especially those in the civil rights and antiwar movements, began to think about their own claims to justice and equality.

LEGACY OF THE SELMA TO MONTGOMERY MARCH

On March 21, two weeks after the violent confrontation on the Edmund Pettis Bridge, activists once again set out to march from Selma to Montgomery. This time, Johnson sent US Army troops and Alabama National Guard forces under federal control to protect the marchers. Led by Dr. Martin Luther King Jr., the protesters walked for more than twelve hours a day. At night, they camped in fields. As they approached Montgomery, more and more people joined them. By the time they reached the State Capitol Building on March 25, the crowd numbered more than twenty-five thousand.

Because of this historic march, in 1996 Congress designated the route between Selma and Montgomery a National Historic Trail—a trail or roadway with historic significance to the United States. In 2015 Congress voted to award the Selma marchers with Congressional Gold Medals—the nation's highest civilian (nonmilitary) honor. On February 24, 2016, President Barack Obama presented the medals to two surviving marchers, John Lewis, a congressional representative from Georgia, and Frederick Reese, a minister from Selma. They accepted the medals on behalf of all the marchers.

Martin Luther King Jr. (*right of center, front*) and his wife, Coretta Scott King (*to his left*) lead a second march from Selma to Montgomery on March 21, 1965, this time with protection of federal troops. The route has since become a National Historic Trail.

In her best-selling book *The Feminine Mystique,* which came out in 1963, author and activist Betty Friedan argued that women deserved more. She said that women who had both children and a career were happier than stay-at-home housewives were. Three years after the book came out, Friedan and other feminists founded the National Organization for Women (NOW). The founders of NOW were frustrated that the US government was not enforcing the part of the Civil Rights Act that forbids discrimination based on sex. Many other discriminatory laws remained as well. These laws barred women from many professions, schools, sports organizations, and political activities. NOW wanted the laws to live up to their promise that women and men have equal chances of being hired and promoted, and of receiving equal pay for equal work. The group's Statement of Purpose began, "We . . . believe that the time has come for a new movement toward true equality for all women in America, and toward a fully equal partnership of the sexes, as part of the world-wide revolution of human rights now taking place within and beyond our national borders."

A second wave of feminism had begun. Over the next twenty years, second-wave feminists won a number of legal victories. For instance, after ongoing pressure by NOW, the US government's Equal Employment Opportunity Commission ruled in 1968 that sex-segregated job ads violated the Civil Rights Act. The help-wanted ads had up until then divided jobs into those for men and those for women, restricting the careers open to women.

Women gained more control over their own bodies in the 1960s and 1970s. One huge development was the birth control pill, introduced in the late 1950s. Much more effective than other types of birth control, the pill was easy to take and put women in control of whether to become pregnant. By 1969 more than 80 percent of married women of childbearing age were using it. In 1973 the Supreme Court decided in *Roe v. Wade* that a woman had a constitutional right to privacy, which included the right to have an abortion. Women could choose to end an unwanted pregnancy safely and legally. The decision was highly controversial at the time and has remained an issue of heated political debate ever since.

Marriage and divorce laws also changed in this era. Previously, to obtain a divorce in many states, a woman had to prove that her husband had abused her,

Passed in 1972, Title IX prohibits discrimination based on sex at schools and universities that receive federal funding. Among other achievements, the law has resulted in increased funding for female athletics programs and the dramatic increase in women and girls' participation in sports.

cheated on her, or deserted her. New no-fault divorce laws allowed people to end their marriages for any reason.

During the 1960s and 1970s, education for women made huge strides. Prestigious universities such as Princeton and Yale began to admit women for the first time in their histories. Title IX was a major victory too. This 1972 federal law forbids sex discrimination by any school or educational program that receives money from the federal government. Most US public and private schools and universities do. Title IX requires schools to treat women fairly in "recruitment, admissions, counseling, financial assistance, athletics, sex-based harassment, treatment of pregnant and parenting students, discipline, single-sex education, and employment." Title IX has been particularly important in expanding opportunities for female athletes. The Women's Sports Foundation reports that since passage of Title IX, girls' participation in high school sports has increased by more than 900 percent.

9

THE FIGHT GOES ON

Thanks to the tireless efforts of feminists, the United States is closer to realizing the bold vision first put forward by Lucy Stone, Elizabeth Cady Stanton, and Susan B. Anthony. According to the National Center for Education Statistics, young women of the twenty-first century are more likely than young men are to receive a bachelor's degree by the end of their twenties. Women and men are equally likely to pursue an advanced degree.

Much work remains. Wage inequality is a reality for American women. In 2017 women were earning eighty cents for every dollar men earned. And the gap is much larger for black and Hispanic women, who make sixty-two cents and fifty-four cents, respectively, for every dollar men earn. In part, this difference is related to occupation and industry. In subtle, sometimes unconscious ways, teachers, parents, and mentors often push women toward traditionally female professions such as nursing, teaching, counseling, and social work. And because women make up most of the workers in these fields, they are relatively low paying. Women who instead pursue careers in high-paying, traditionally male fields—such as manufacturing, banking, and engineering—usually earn less money than their male counterparts do. They are also less likely to get raises and promotions, a phenomenon known as the glass ceiling. And while women have entered politics in greater numbers over the years, women hold only one in five seats in the US Congress.

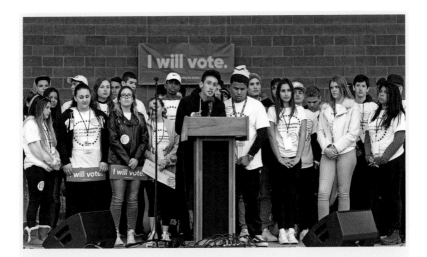

Student survivors of school shootings address a Vote for Our Lives rally in Littleton, Colorado, in April 2018. The Vote for Our Lives program encourages Americans to cast ballots for candidates who support stronger gun laws.

Women with families also face discrimination. It is illegal to discriminate against women because they are or may become pregnant, yet employers do it all the time. Bosses often decide not to hire or promote capable, highly qualified women because they assume that women are more committed to their families than to their jobs. They assume female workers will quit their jobs when they become mothers. Many employers do not want to give new mothers paid maternity leave or allow them to reduce their work hours when their children are young. So they hire or promote a man instead.

THE NEW FIGHT FOR SUFFRAGE

The fight for true equality for women continues, and so does the fight for access to the ballot—for both women and men. In the twenty-first century, voting rights face a new threat. In the 2010 midterm elections, Republicans won control of many state governments, winning governorships and control of state legislatures. They also gained a majority of seats in the US House of Representatives and gained six seats in the US Senate, edging closer to a majority there. With increased political power, Republican lawmakers began to make new laws about voting rights. For example, Republican legislators in forty-one states introduced 180 bills designed to reduce voter fraud. Twenty-five of these laws passed, affecting voters in nineteen states. Researchers have investigated the issue of voter fraud, including the idea that people pretend to be someone else at voting stations or that noncitizen immigrants vote illegally. They have found no evidence of widespread voter fraud. The real reason behind these laws, critics say, is to make it more difficult for women, minorities, young people, and the poor to vote. And since these Americans tend to vote Democratic, the laws are designed to reduce Democratic voter turnout and improve Republican chances of winning elections.

Republicans have also pushed for new proof-of-citizenship laws. These laws require that potential voters prove they are US citizens before they register to vote rather than simply signing a statement that swears to citizenship. In Kansas a law passed in 2011 required new voters to present a driver's license, birth certificate, or passport. If new voters were born outside of the United States, naturalization papers (documents proving US citizenship) were required. The League of Women Voters of Kansas and other advocacy groups challenged Kansas's proof-of-citizenship law. They argued that it prevented many eligible women and men from registering to vote. Not all adults have a driver's license, for example. And 7 percent of eligible voters—about 16.8 million people—do not have a birth certificate, passport, or naturalization papers. Obtaining these documents can be difficult, time-consuming, and costly. In 2018 an official copy of a birth certificate cost from $8 to $25. A passport cost $110, and copies of naturalization papers cost $345. This often discourages a significant number of people from registering to vote.

The Kansas law had a devastating effect on voter registration campaigns. When the League of Women Voters tried to help young adults register to vote at Washburn University in Topeka, only seventy-five voter applications were approved out of four hundred applicants. Many of the applicants were not willing or able to show volunteers the proper documents. Others decided not to go through with the registration once they found out how much time and effort it would take. Between 2011 and 2016, Kansas officials rejected more than thirty thousand voter registration applications because they did not provide the information required under the proof-of-citizenship law. In 2018 a Kansas judge overturned the proof-of-citizenship law. Because the State of Kansas could not prove that noncitizens voting was a problem, the judge ruled that the harm caused by the law was much greater than its benefit. Similar laws in other states are also being challenged in the courts.

In thirty-four states, legislatures passed voter identification laws, which require people to show identification before voting. The requirements vary from state to state. Some states accept a non-photo ID, such as a bank statement with the voter's name and address. Stricter states require a government-issued photo ID, such as a driver's license, state-issued identification card, military ID, or Indian tribal ID.

Evidence shows that ID laws are particularly burdensome on women, the young, the poor, immigrants, people of color, people with disabilities, senior citizens, and transgender women and men. Many women change their last name when they get married or divorced. If the name on the voter registration doesn't match the ID, a divorced woman who has changed her name might be turned away at the polls. Transgender Americans face similar obstacles. They may have changed their first name unofficially, to match their gender identity, but lack ID to confirm the change. And some states do not accept student IDs, which may be the only type of identification a young voter has. Texas drew criticism with a voter ID law that rejects student ID cards as a valid form of identification but accepts gun licenses. This law clearly disadvantages college students, who tend to vote for Democrats, and favors gun owners, who tend to vote Republican.

A driver's license is the most common form of ID in the United States. So people who do not drive are disproportionately affected by ID laws. Nondrivers include people with disabilities and people who cannot afford a car. Many of these people are black and Hispanic, and blacks and Hispanics tend to vote for Democrats.

Estimates for the number of eligible voters without an ID range from 1 percent to 11 percent—between 2.4 and 26.4 million people. Getting the proper ID can be difficult. The offices that issue them often have limited daytime hours only. They often have long wait times for service. They may be difficult to get to by public transportation, which is the only transportation option for many poor people. Online forms may overwhelm some people, and not all potential voters have internet access in their homes. Language barriers, for people who do not speak or write English, may get in the way. And an ID can be expensive. Many potential voters face too many obstacles to get an ID, so they simply don't vote.

VOTER PURGES

As a way to stay current, counties routinely remove names from lists of eligible voters. Known as purging the voter rolls, the idea is to remove the names of voters who have died or moved to another state or voting district. However, some eligible voters are removed from the rolls during voter purges. When they show up to the polls, they are not allowed to vote.

To influence elections, political parties also use a tactic called voter caging. They send out do-not-forward mass mailings to registered voters in neighborhoods that are heavily populated by members of the opposing party. If the post office returns that piece of mail as undeliverable, the party can then challenge that voter's registration. Based on this challenge, the state might then purge that person from the voter rolls. This unfairly disenfranchises women who have changed their names (after marriage or divorce) without notifying the post office, people who have recently moved and not yet registered to vote at their new addresses, and those who move often, such as college students and poor people who cannot afford a permanent home. Voter caging is legal in many states. However, it is often racially motivated, used to prevent people of color from voting. This is a violation of the Voting Rights Act of 1965 and has been challenged in court.

The State of Ohio tries to keep its voter rolls up to date by mailing a notice to all voters who have not voted for two years. They must return this notice, confirming that they are still eligible to vote in the district where they are registered. If they do not return the notice and do not vote within the next four years, they are purged from the rolls. In 2010 US Navy veteran and Ohio resident Larry Harmon chose not to vote in the midterm elections. This was not unusual for him. He usually votes only in presidential elections. The State of Ohio mailed him a postcard asking him to confirm that his address had not changed. Harmon did not remember receiving the postcard. In 2012 he did not like either presidential candidate and once again stayed home on Election Day. Because he had not voted in two elections, Ohio purged him from the rolls. Harmon was unaware that he'd been purged until he tried to vote in 2015. Furious at being denied his chance to vote, Harmon sued the state. "I earned the right to vote," Harmon said. "Whether I use it or not is up to my personal discretion. They don't take away my right to buy a gun if I don't buy a gun." Harmon's case *(Husted v. A. Philip Randolph Institute)* went to the US Supreme Court, which in 2018 ruled that Ohio's voter-purge law is constitutional. Critics charge that the law robs people of the right to vote.

LONG LINES AND LIMITED HOURS

Some states work hard to increase voter turnout. Their leaders believe that democracy is strongest when people participate. So these states try to make it easy to vote. Early voting is a period of a week or more before Election Day. During this time, voters can cast ballots at various polling places. This particularly helps poor, elderly, and disabled women and men, who may have difficulty making it to the polls on Election Day. For instance, they may not have a car or access to reliable public transportation. Early voting gives all voters more flexibility and so increases voter turnout. As of 2017, thirty-seven states and the District of Columbia offer early voting. Some states also make it easier to vote by allowing new voters to register and cast their ballots on the same day.

Other states have made voting less convenient. In nineteen states, employers are not required to give workers time off to vote, making it difficult for some workers to fit in a trip to the polls during the workday. Other states do not set aside enough money to pay for polling places and equipment. So these states shut down some polling places or simply don't have enough polling places to meet voter demand. In these places, voters have to travel long distances to an out-of-the-way polling place. Many voters, especially those without cars, are unable or unwilling to go that far. Too few polling places also means long lines. Some voters in Charlotte, North Carolina; Las Vegas, Nevada; and New York City had to wait up to two hours or more to vote in the 2016 presidential election. Many voters cannot wait that long. They have health problems, kids, jobs, and other obligations that keep them from spending several hours in line. Studies show that people who have to wait in long lines are less likely to vote in future elections as well. Studies also show that these obstacles to voting disproportionately affect the poor and people of color.

Some states, including Alabama—where these voters wait in long lines on Election Day—have purposely reduced the number of polling places, which makes the remaining polling places more crowded. Faced with long lines such as this one, some voters get discouraged and choose not to vote. Studies show that if people have trouble voting in one election, they are less likely to vote in future elections.

GERRYMANDERING

Gerrymandering is a powerful way of weakening one political party's votes and strengthening another party's votes. Gerrymandering occurs when officials divide a state, county, or city into voting districts to favor one political party over the other. Officials might divide a state so that certain districts with high turnout rates are lumped together. Or they might shape districts so that black voters make up a minority rather than a majority of voters. Based on what political leaders know about how people vote, a gerrymandered district usually ensures an outcome that a party wants.

A BLOW TO THE VOTING RIGHTS ACT

A provision of the Voting Rights Act of 1965 said that states and counties with a history of racial discrimination in voting had to get permission from the Justice Department before changing any voting laws or practices. If the federal government believed that a proposed law would harm the voting rights of particular racial groups, that law could not be enacted. In 2013, in *Shelby County v. Holder*, the Supreme Court threw out this part of the Voting Rights Act.

Chief Justice John Roberts, writing the majority opinion, acknowledged that the Voting Rights Act had been necessary in its day and had been very successful at "redressing racial discrimination and integrating the voting process." But Roberts also argued that it was wrong to interfere in the lawmaking practices of certain places just because their citizens had been racist at the time the Voting Rights Act was enacted. He said it was a violation of the rights of the states to punish them "based on 40-year-old facts having no logical relationship to the present day." The country had changed a great deal since the 1960s, he argued.

Four of the justices disagreed. Writing a strong dissent, Justice Ruth Bader Ginsburg (*above*) argued that "throwing out preclearance [federal approval] when it has worked and is continuing to work to stop discriminatory changes is like throwing away your umbrella in a rainstorm because you are not getting wet."

Following the ruling, many states—including several that hadn't been required to get federal approval under the Voting Rights Act—rushed to make changes in their voting policies. Across the country, nearly one thousand polling places were closed, many of them in communities with large African American populations. A number of states reduced or eliminated early voting, implemented voter ID laws, eliminated online voter registration, implemented voter purges, and made other changes likely to reduce voter turnout.

Every ten years, the United States takes a census to count all the people living in the nation. After the census, state legislatures or commissions draw new voting districts to ensure that all districts have roughly equal numbers of people. By gerrymandering the districts, parties that control state legislatures can rig the system, ensuring that their party has an unfair advantage in elections for the next ten years.

Gerrymandering is illegal if it is used to weaken or cancel out the votes of racial minority groups. In the twenty-first century, many states appear to have used it that way, but racially based gerrymandering is also difficult to prove in court. The courts have yet to decide whether gerrymandering is illegal if it is partisan—favors one political party over another in elections. As of 2018, several important cases that will determine this question were pending in the courts.

SEIZE THAT BALLOT!

Voting restrictions make it harder for some people to access the ballot. But many eligible voters simply choose not to exercise their right to vote. Because of voting restrictions and voter apathy, the United States trails most other wealthy democracies in voter turnout. Less than 56 percent of American adults voted in the 2016 presidential election.

Women make up a majority of American voters. In every election since 1964, more women than men have showed up at the polls. In the 2010s, female voters exceeded male voters by several million. But women's commitment to voting varies by age. Young women are less likely to vote than older women are. Less than half (46 percent) of women aged eighteen to twenty-nine voted in 2016, as opposed to 72 percent of women aged sixty-five to seventy-four. Men have a similar pattern.

Voting is key to democracy, so voter registration campaigns are a major focus of political activism. In the lead-up to the 2018 midterm elections, many groups made a push to register new voters, especially young voters, and to encourage voters to turn out on Election Day. In 2018 former first lady Michelle Obama participated in an initiative called When We All Vote. She appeared in a YouTube video and spent a week on the road encouraging people to register to vote. "There's too much at stake to sit on the sidelines, not just in this election, but in every election, and we need your help right now," she said.

GERRYMANDERING UP CLOSE

To see how gerrymandering works, imagine a city of fifty voters getting ready to vote for members of the state legislature (Figure 1). Let's say that by law, the city has five voting districts of ten people each. The Orange Party has 60 percent of the voters, and 40 percent belong to the Purple Party. If the voters were divided into districts according to exact party preference, the Orange Party would win 60 percent of the seats in the legislature and the Purple Party would win 40 percent. Then each party's representation in the government would be proportional to its support in the population (Figure 2).

But by drawing up districts in different ways, the voting can have a very different outcome. Let's say the Orange Party is in charge of drawing the districts. It might configure them so that Orange voters have a majority in all five districts (Figure 3). Then the Orange Party would win all the seats in the legislature. This would be unfair to Purple Party voters. They would have no representatives in the government. Their votes would be canceled out.

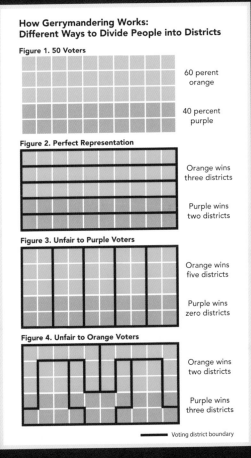

How Gerrymandering Works:
Different Ways to Divide People into Districts

Figure 1. 50 Voters

60 perent orange

40 percent purple

Figure 2. Perfect Representation

Orange wins three districts

Purple wins two districts

Figure 3. Unfair to Purple Voters

Orange wins five districts

Purple wins zero districts

Figure 4. Unfair to Orange Voters

Orange wins two districts

Purple wins three districts

— Voting district boundary

Imagine that the Purple Party divides the districts as shown in Figure 4. Then their party wins in three districts and the Orange Party wins in only two. This is unfair to the Orange Party supporters, whose representation in government (40 percent of the seats) would be diluted, or less than their proportion of the population (60 percent).

Celebrities such as Beyoncé, media outlets such as MTV, and corporations such as Walmart participated in voter registration campaigns in 2018. The group NextGen America, founded by billionaire Tom Steyer, poured money into a large-scale campaign targeting college students in swing states (states that sometimes go to Republicans and sometimes to Democrats). NextGen America sent more than seven hundred full- and part-time organizers and student volunteers to college campuses. Their goals were to register half a million new young voters in 2018.

Grassroots social justice movements also inspired more Americans to vote. After the 2016 election of Donald Trump as president, a racially and ethnically diverse group of female activists organized a Women's March on Washington, DC. Millions of women—and men—across the country participated in sister marches. The marchers wanted to speak out against Trump's racist, sexist, and anti-immigrant rhetoric. Afterward, Women's March became an advocacy group. It started Power to the Polls, an online and text-based system to help citizens register to vote, find their polling places, and learn when and if early voting is available where they live.

VOTING AROUND THE WORLD

Compared to voters in other parts of the world, Americans are relatively poor at turning out to vote. The United States ranks twenty-sixth out of thirty-two democratic countries in voter participation. One reason is the US voter registration system: the United States places the burden on citizens to register themselves. In most other democratic nations, the government ensures that all citizens are registered to vote. For instance, Canada automatically adds people to the rolls when they turn eighteen or when they become Canadian citizens. If they move, they remain on the rolls.

Some countries go even further and require all citizens to vote or at least show up at the polls, or they may be fined. Countries that enforce compulsory voting include Argentina, Australia, Belgium, Brazil, and Singapore.

This sticker says "I Voted" in thirteen languages. A 2006 federal law requires election officials to provide foreign-language ballots for US citizens whose first language is not English.

Tamika Mallory, national cochair for the Women's March, said, "People should be as frustrated and as angry as they want to be. They should be visibly in the streets, but they must take that anger and frustration to the polls, and they cannot go to the polls alone. They must make sure they take their families and communities with them."

The #MeToo movement has also increased women's political activism. In 2017 the movement seized the social media spotlight, as women across the nation and around the globe shared stories of sexual violence, sexual harassment, and sexual discrimination. Many women in the #MeToo campaign mobilized voters, encouraging them to cast their ballots for candidates who will fight for women's equality and safety.

A group of students from Marjory Stoneman Douglas High School in Parkland, Florida, led another prominent voter registration campaign. Seventeen people died in a mass shooting at the school in 2018. Parkland students organized a march, hoping to increase support for gun control and other measures to prevent school shootings.

Later, they decided to conduct a nationwide tour to register young people to vote. The senior class president, Jaclyn Corin, said, "On March 24, we gathered together, we marched, and we demanded a change. But the only way that change is truly going to be enacted is through voting."

To win the ballot, hundreds of Americans have suffered threats, humiliation, arrest, jail, force-feeding, violence, and even death. But the ballot is only as powerful as the will of the people to use it. That is why sixteen-year-old Estefania Alba started talking to other teens about voting before she could vote herself. Alba, from Queens, New York, explained to *Teen Vogue* what voting means to her: "At a young age, my older sister taught me to stand up for what I believe in. She taught me that I should always vocalize my opinion even if there are other voices louder than mine. So, in 2020 when I get to vote for the first time, I won't only be voting for myself. I will also be voting for my family and my community. That's why educating other teens on how to use our voices to speak up and be heard is so significant." Young people need to understand their power, Alba says. They can contribute to the political discussions happening in this country, vote for their representatives, and shape the future of their communities. "We, as youth, matter."

THREATS FROM ABROAD

The 2016 presidential election revealed that American democracy is vulnerable to attacks from abroad. Prior to the election, hackers tied to the Russian government infiltrated the computers of the Democratic National Committee and the campaign of Hillary Clinton, the Democratic presidential candidate. The hackers released tens of thousands of committee emails to stir up conflict within the party. Russian operatives also hacked into Republican Party computers but did not release Republican documents or emails.

Russian hackers also conducted an elaborate social media campaign. They illegally paid for thousands of political ads, especially in the crucial battleground states of Michigan and Wisconsin. Russian operatives spread false information and provoked division on social media. They spread fake news articles—on hot-button topics such as immigration and the Black Lives Matter movement—designed to mislead and anger American voters.

Russian agents also attempted to hack into voting machines in at least twenty-one states. According to US intelligence agencies, no vote totals were changed, but Russians may have gained access to lists of voter names and addresses. Donald Trump won the 2016 election, and many think that Russian influence helped him win. The US Central Intelligence Agency thinks that Russia wanted Trump to win because he is much more supportive of Russian president Vladimir Putin than Hillary Clinton is.

Russians with ties to Putin spent millions of dollars trying to influence the 2018 US midterm elections as well. They posted inflammatory messages on social media on both sides of controversial topics, including immigration, gun control, race relations, and women's rights. According to FBI special agent David Holt, "The [Russian] conspiracy has a strategic goal, which continues to this day, to sow division and discord in the U.S. political system."

Voting machines continue to be vulnerable to hackers. To prevent successful vote tampering in the future, US election officials and other concerned citizens stress the importance of always having paper as well as electronic ballots. That way, if electronic voting machines are compromised, paper ballots can be counted to ensure a fair election.

GLOSSARY

abolition movement: the organized effort to end slavery in the United States. Many members of the abolition movement were also active in the fight for woman suffrage.

civil rights: the freedoms and rights that a person has as a member of a nation. In the United States, at different times, some groups have been deprived of their civil rights, such as the right to vote.

Fifteenth Amendment: an amendment to the US Constitution saying that federal and state governments cannot bar citizens from voting based on race. Ratified in 1870, the amendment was designed to assure voting rights for black men following the Civil War.

Fourteenth Amendment: an amendment to the US Constitution that forbids states to deny rights to any US citizen. It also states that all citizens are entitled to equal protection of the law. Ratified in 1868, the amendment was designed to protect the rights of former slaves.

franchise: the right to vote. Those who are deprived of the right to vote are disenfranchised.

gerrymandering: dividing an area into election districts in a way that gives one political party a majority in many districts while limiting the strength of the opposition party in those districts

Jim Crow: practices, laws, and institutions that discriminated against black Americans in the southern United States from the mid-nineteenth century until the mid-twentieth century. These laws and practices included efforts to keep black people from voting.

Nineteenth Amendment: an amendment to the US Constitution that grants voting rights to women. The amendment was ratified in 1920.

Prohibition: a period in US history, between 1920 and 1933, when it was illegal to manufacture, transport, or sell alcoholic beverages in the United States. Many of the people who fought for Prohibition also fought for woman suffrage.

Reconstruction: from 1865 until 1877, when the US government reorganized and reestablished the governments of states that had previously seceded from the Union. US troops occupied the former Confederate states during those years. Southern states could not rejoin the Union until they had guaranteed voting rights for black men, elected new leaders, and created new state constitutions.

suffrage: the right to vote. American suffragists used the term *woman suffrage* to describe their goal of attaining voting rights for women.

temperance: moderation in or rejection of the use of alcoholic beverages. Many members of the US temperance movement also fought for woman suffrage.

Thirteenth Amendment: an amendment to the US Constitution that abolished slavery in the United States. The amendment was adopted in 1865, during the last year of the Civil War.

voter suppression: deliberate efforts to influence the outcome of elections by discouraging or preventing specific groups from voting. In the mid-twentieth century, some election officials used literacy tests and poll taxes to keep black Americans from voting. In the twenty-first century, voter suppression tactics include gerrymandering and restrictive voter ID and proof-of-citizenship requirements.

SOURCE NOTES

5   Mary Walton, *A Woman's Crusade: Alice Paul and the Battle for the Ballot* (New York: Palgrave Macmillan, 2010), 76.

6   Walton, 76.

6   "Failure Is Impossible: Susan B. Anthony in Her Own Words," *Booknotes*, March 5, 1995, http://www.booknotes.org/Watch/63336-1/Lynn-Sherr.

11   Elizabeth Frost and Kathryn Cullen-DuPont, *Woman Suffrage in America: An Eyewitness History* (New York: Facts on File, 1992), 41.

13   Elizabeth Cady Stanton, *Eighty Years and More: Reminiscences* (London: T. Fisher Unwin, 1898), 20–21.

15   Elisabeth Griffith, *In Her Own Right: The Life of Elizabeth Cady Stanton* (New York: Oxford University Press, 1984), 37.

16   Stanton, *Eighty Years*, 147–148.

16   Elizabeth Cady Stanton and Susan B. Anthony Papers Project, "Declaration of Sentiments and Resolutions," Rutgers University, last modified August 2010, http://ecssba.rutgers.edu/docs/seneca.html.

17   Stanton, *Eighty Years*, 147–148.

17   Griffith, *In Her Own Right*, 58.

18   Andrea Moore Kerr, *Lucy Stone: Speaking Out for Equality* (New Brunswick, NJ: Rutgers University Press, 1992), 8.

18   Kerr, 50.

19   Kerr, 55.

19   Kerr, 55.

19   Kerr, 55.

19   Kerr, 52.

21   Lynn Sherr, *Failure Is Impossible: Susan B. Anthony in Her Own Words* (New York: Times Books, 1995), 19–20.

21   Kerr, *Lucy Stone*, 60.

21   Kerr, 61.

22   Kathleen Barry, *Susan B. Anthony: A Biography of a Singular Feminist* (New York: New York University Press, 1988), 81.

23   Griffith, *In Her Own Right*, 94.

23   Griffith, 94.

23–24   Kerr, *Lucy Stone*, 86.

24   Rutgers University Press, "About This Book," Rutgers University Press, accessed November 8, 2018, https://www.rutgersuniversitypress.org /lucy-stone/9780813518602.

24   Griffith, *In Her Own Right*, 91.

24   Griffith.

26   "13th Amendment to the U.S. Constitution," Library of Congress, last modified September 18, 2018, https://www.loc.gov/rr/program/bib /ourdocs/13thamendment.html.

27   "Civil War and Reconstruction, 1861–1877," Library of Congress, accessed October 16, 2018, http://www.loc.gov/teachers/classroommaterials /presentationsandactivities/presentations/timeline/civilwar/freedmen/mott .html.

27   Daniel R. Vollaro, "Lincoln, Stowe, and the 'Little Woman/Great War' Story: The Making, and Breaking, of a Great American Anecdote," *Journal of the Abraham Lincoln Association* 30, no. 1 (Winter 2009): 18–34, http://hdl.handle.net/2027/spo.2629860.0030.104.

28   Faye E. Dudden, *Fighting Chance: The Struggle over Woman Suffrage and Black Suffrage in Reconstruction America* (New York: Oxford University Press, 2011), 62.

29   Kerr, *Lucy Stone*, 122.

29   Dudden, *Fighting Chance*, 73.

29   Dudden, 96.

30   Elizabeth Cady Stanton, Susan B. Anthony, and Matilda Joslyn Gage, eds., *History of Woman Suffrage*, vol. 1 (New York: Fowler and Wells, 1881), 115–116.

34   "U.S. Constitution: 15th Amendment," Cornell Law School, accessed October 16, 2018, https://www.law.cornell.edu/constitution/amendmentxv.

34   Frederick Douglass, *Frederick Douglass on Women's Rights* (New York: Da Capo, 1976), 87–88.

34   Douglass, 87–88.

34   Douglass, 88.

35   Douglass, 88.

35   Douglass, 89.

35   Douglass, 90.

35   Dudden, *Fighting Chance*, 181.

38   "Amendment XIX: Women's Right to Vote," Constitution Center, accessed October 16, 2018, https://constitutioncenter.org/interactive-constitution /amendments/amendment-xix.

40   Judith E. Harper, "Susan B. Anthony and Elizabeth Cady Stanton," *PBS*, accessed October 25, 2018, https://www.pbs.org/stantonanthony/resources/index.html?body=biography.html.

40   Barbara Goldsmith, *Other Powers: The Age of Suffrage, Spiritualism, and the Scandalous Victoria Woodhull* (New York: Alfred A. Knopf, 1998), 253.

41   Jane Rhodes, *Mary Ann Shadd Cary: The Black Press and Protest in the Nineteenth Century* (Bloomington: Indiana University Press, 1999), 195.

43   Goldsmith, *Other Powers*, 303.

44   Jean H. Baker, *Sisters: The Lives of America's Suffragists* (New York: Farrar, Straus and Giroux, 2006), 143.

45   Baker, 142.

47   Marjorie Spruill Wheeler, ed., *One Woman, One Vote: Rediscovering the Woman Suffrage Movement* (Troutdale, OR: NewSage, 1995), 119.

51   T. A. Larson, "Woman Suffrage in Western America," *Utah Historical Quarterly* 38, no. 1 (Winter 1970): 7–19, http://digitallibrary.utah.gov/awweb/awarchive?type=file&item=34303.

51   Rebecca J. Mead, *How the Vote Was Won: Woman Suffrage in the Western United States, 1868–1914* (New York: New York University Press, 2004), 56.

52   Lynne Cheney, "It All Began in Wyoming," *American Heritage*, accessed November 8, 2018, https://web.archive.org/web/20090426221347/http://www.americanheritage.com/articles/magazine/ah/1973/3/1973_3_62.shtml.

53   Mead, 65.

55   Jean Bickmore White, "Woman's Place Is in the Constitution: The Struggle for Equal Rights in Utah in 1895," *Utah Historical Quarterly* 42, no. 4 (Fall 1974): 344–369, http://digitallibrary.utah.gov/awweb/awarchive?type=file&item=34304.

55   White.

59   Walton, *Woman's Crusade*, 3.

62   Walton, 28.

63   Diane Atkinson, *Rise Up, Women! The Remarkable Lives of the Suffragettes* (London: Bloomsbury, 2018), 180.

64   Walton, *Woman's Crusade*, 29.

64   "Alice Paul Describes Force Feeding," Library of Congress, accessed October 16, 2018, https://www.loc.gov/item/rbcmiller003904.

65   "Photo, Print, Drawing," Library of Congress, accessed November 8, 2018https://www.loc.gov/photos/?fa=contributor%3Aharris+%26+ewing%7Csubject%3Awomen%27s+suffrage.

67   Walton, *Woman's Crusade*, 79.

68   Walton, 141.

68   Walton, 142.

68   "National Woman's Party Fine Art Collection," NWP, accessed January 22, 2018, https://nationalwomansparty.pastperfectonline.com/webobject /428FD076-6BE2-48AE-997C-786843535729.

69   Doris Stevens, *Jailed for Freedom* (Troutdale, OR: NewSage, 1995), 57–58.

69   Bethanee Bemis, "Mr. President, How Long Must Women Wait for Liberty?," *Smithsonian*, January 12, 2017, https://www.smithsonianmag .com/smithsonian-institution/scrap-suffrage-history-180961780/.

70   Stevens, *Jailed*, 62.

71   Wheeler, *One Woman, One Vote*, 299.

72   Wheeler, 69–70.

72   Wheeler, 74.

72   Wheeler, 74.

73   "Rankin, Jeannette," United States House of Representatives, accessed September 20, 2018, http://history.house.gov/People/Detail/20147.

73   "Rankin."

73   "Rankin."

74   Wheeler, 95.

76   Wheeler, 132.

76   Jill Diane Zahniser and Amelia R. Fry, *Alice Paul, Claiming Power* (New York: Oxford University Press, 2014), 306.

77   Zahniser and Fry, 224.

78   Frost and Cullen-DuPont, *Woman Suffrage in America*, 332–333.

78   Frost and Cullen-DuPont, 335.

79   Frost and Cullen-DuPont, 351.

80   Walton, *Woman's Crusade,* 245.

83   DeNeen L. Brown, "Civil Rights Crusader Fannie Lou Hamer Defied Men—and Presidents—Who Tried to Silence Her," *Washington Post*, October 6, 2017, https://www.washingtonpost.com/news/retropolis /wp/2017/10/06/civil-rights-crusader-fannie-lou-hamer-defied-men-and -presidents-who-tried-to-silence-her/?utm_term=.37092439b936.

83   Brown.

84   "Fannie Lou Hamer," *American Experience*, accessed November 8, 2018, https://www.pbs.org/wgbh/americanexperience/features/freedomsummer -hamer/.

85   Lyndon Baines Johnson, "President Johnson's Special Message to the Congress: The American Promise," LBJ Presidential Library, March 15, 1965, http://www.lbjlibrary.org/lyndon-baines-johnson/speeches-films /president-johnsons-special-message-to-the-congress-the-american-promise.

88   "The National Organization for Women's 1966 Statement of Purpose," NOW, accessed November 8, 2018, http://www.now.org/history/purpos66 .html.

89   "Title IX and Sex Discrimination," US Department of Education, last modified April 2015, https://www2.ed.gov/about/offices/list/ocr/docs /tix_dis.html?exp=0.

95   Nina Totenberg, "Supreme Court Upholds Controversial Ohio Voter-Purge Law," National Public Radio, June 11, 2018, https://www.npr .org/2018/06/11/618870982/supreme-court-upholds-controversial-ohio -voter-purge-law.

97   "Shelby County, Alabama v. Holder, Attorney General, et al," Supreme Court, October 2012, https://www.supremecourt.gov/opinions/12pdf/12 -96_6k47.pdf.

97   "Shelby County."

97   "Shelby County."

98   Katie Kindelan, "Michelle Obama to Hit the Road to Register Voters before the Midterms," *ABC News*, August 6, 2018, https://abcnews.go.com/GMA /News/michelle-obama-hit-road-register-voters-midterms /story?id=57054022.

101   Emanuella Grinberg, "What's Next for #MeToo after Kavanaugh's Confirmation," CNN, October 14, 2018, https://edition.cnn.com /2018/10/13/us/kavanaugh-whats-next-metoo/index.html.

102   Eliott C. McLaughlin, "Parkland Students Will Tour the Nation to Register Voters and Demand Change," CNN, June 4, 2018, https://edition.cnn. com/2018/06/04/us/parkland-student-road-to-change-tour/index.html.

102   Estefania Alba, "I'm 16 and Campaigning for Other Teens to Vote," *Teen Vogue*, October 9, 2017, https://www.teenvogue.com/story/teen-voting -importance.

103   Adam Goldman, "Justice Dept. Accuses Russians of Interfering in Midterm Elections," *New York Times*, October 19, 2018, https://www.nytimes .com/2018/10/19/us/politics/russia-interference-midterm-elections.html.

SELECTED BIBLIOGRAPHY

Alexander, Thomas G. "An Experiment in Progressive Legislation: The Granting of Woman Suffrage in Utah in 1870." *Utah Historical Quarterly* 38, no. 1 (Winter 1970): 20–30, http://digitallibrary.utah.gov/awweb/awarchive?type=file&item=34303.

Barry, Kathleen. *Susan B. Anthony: A Biography of a Singular Feminist.* New York: New York University Press, 1988.

Blatch, Harriot Stanton, and Alma Lutz. *Challenging Years: The Memoirs of Harriot Stanton Blatch.* New York: Putnam, 1940.

Catt, Carrie Chapman, and Nettie Rogers Shuler. *Woman Suffrage and Politics.* New York: Scribner, 1923.

Chappel, Bill. "Judge Tosses Kansas' Proof-of-Citizenship Voter Law and Rebukes Sec. of State Kobach." *National Public Radio,* June 19, 2018. https://www.npr.org/2018/06/19/621304260/judge-tosses-kansas-proof-of-citizenship-voter-law-and-rebukes-sec-of-state-koba.

Chira, Susan. "The Women's March Became a Movement. What's Next?" *New York Times,* January 20, 2018. https://www.nytimes.com/2018/01/20/us/womens-march-metoo.html.

Desilver, Drew. "U.S. Trails Most Developed Countries in Voter Turnout." Pew Research Center, May 21, 2018. http://www.pewresearch.org/fact-tank/2018/05/21/u-s-voter-turnout-trails-most-developed-countries/.

Douglass, Frederick. *Frederick Douglass on Women's Rights.* New York: Da Capo, 1976.

Dudden, Faye E. *Fighting Chance: The Struggle over Woman Suffrage and Black Suffrage in Reconstruction America.* New York: Oxford University Press, 2011.

Frost, Elizabeth, and Kathryn Cullen-DuPont. *Woman Suffrage in America: An Eyewitness History.* New York: Facts on File, 1992.

Giele, Janet Zollinger. *Two Paths to Women's Equality: Temperance, Suffrage, and the Origins of Modern Feminism.* New York: Twayne, 1995.

Goldsmith, Barbara. *Other Powers: The Age of Suffrage, Spiritualism, and the Scandalous Victoria Woodhull.* New York: Alfred A. Knopf, 1998.

Griffith, Elisabeth. *In Her Own Right: The Life of Elizabeth Cady Stanton.* New York: Oxford University Press, 1984.

Ingraham, Christopher. "New Evidence That Voter ID Laws 'Skew Democracy' in Favor of White Republicans." *Washington Post,* February 4, 2016. https://www.washingtonpost.com/news/wonk/wp/2016/02/04/new-evidence-that-voter-id-laws-skew-democracy-in-favor-of-white-republicans/.

———. "This Is the Best Explanation of Gerrymandering You Will Ever See." *Washington Post,* March 1, 2015. https://www.washingtonpost.com/news/wonk/wp/2015/03/01/this-is-the-best-explanation-of-gerrymandering-you-will-ever-see/?noredirect=on&utm_term=.49ad94e760cb.

Kerr, Andrea Moore. *Lucy Stone: Speaking Out for Equality.* New Brunswick, NJ: Rutgers University Press, 1992.

Kraditor, Aileen S. *The Ideas of the Woman Suffrage Movement: 1890–1920.* New York: W. W. Norton, 1981.

Larson, T. A. "Woman Suffrage in Western America." *Utah Historical Quarterly* 38, no. 1 (Winter 1970): 7–19. http://digitallibrary.utah.gov/awweb/awarchive?type=file&item=34303.

Marilley, Suzanne M. *Woman Suffrage and the Origins of Liberal Feminism in the United States, 1820–1920.* Cambridge, MA: Harvard University Press, 1996.

Massie, Michael A. "Reform Is Where You Find It: The Roots of Woman Suffrage in Wyoming." *Annals of Wyoming* 62, no. 1 (Spring 1990): 2–22. http://archive.org/details/annalsofwyom621231990wyom.

Mead, Rebecca J. *How the Vote Was Won: Woman Suffrage in the Western United States, 1868–1914.* New York: New York University Press, 2004.

Overton, Spencer. *Stealing Democracy: The New Politics of Voter Suppression.* New York: W. W. Norton, 2006.

Sherr, Lynn. *Failure Is Impossible: Susan B. Anthony in Her Own Words.* New York: Times Books, 1995.

Specia, Megan. "Overlooked No More: How Mary Ann Shadd Cary Shook Up the Abolitionist Movement." *New York Times,* June 6, 2018. https://mobile.nytimes.com/2018/06/06/obituaries/mary-ann-shadd-cary-abolitionist-overlooked.html?smid=fb-nytimes&smtyp=cur.

Stevens, Doris. *Jailed for Freedom.* Troutdale, OR: NewSage, 1995.

Walton, Mary. *A Woman's Crusade: Alice Paul and the Battle for the Ballot.* New York: Palgrave Macmillan, 2010.

White, Jean Bickmore. "Woman's Place Is in the Constitution: The Struggle for Equal Rights in Utah in 1895." *Utah Historical Quarterly* 42, no. 4 (Fall 1974): 344–369. http://digitallibrary.utah.gov/awweb/awarchive?type=file&item=34304.

Willard, Frances E. *How I Learned to Ride the Bicycle: Reflections of an Influential 19th Century Woman.* Sunnyvale, CA: Fair Oaks, 1991.

FURTHER INFORMATION

Anderson, Carol. *One Person, No Vote: How Voter Suppression Is Destroying Our Democracy.* New York: Bloomsbury, 2018.

Atkinson, Diane. *Rise Up Women! The Remarkable Lives of the Suffragettes.* New York: Bloomsbury, 2018.

Berman, Ari. *Give Us the Ballot: The Modern Struggle for Voting Rights in America.* New York: Picador, 2016.

Carmon, Irin, and Shana Knizhnik. *Notorious RBG: The Life and Times of Ruth Bader Ginsburg.* New York: HarperCollins, 2015.

Clift, Eleanor. *Founding Sisters and the Nineteenth Amendment.* Hoboken, NJ: John Wiley & Sons, 2003.

Colman, Penny. *Elizabeth Cady Stanton and Susan B. Anthony: A Friendship That Changed the World.* New York: Henry Holt, 2011.

Conkling, Winifred. *Votes for Women: American Suffragists and the Battle for the Ballot.* Chapel Hill, NY: Algonquin Young Readers, 2018.

Edge, Laura. *We Stand as One: The International Ladies Garment Workers Strike, New York, 1909.* Minneapolis: Twenty-First Century Books, 2011.

Frazer, Coral Celeste. *Economic Inequality: The American Dream under Siege.* Minneapolis: Twenty-First Century Books, 2018.

Higgins, Nadia Abushanab. *Feminism: Reinventing the F-Word.* Minneapolis: Twenty-First Century Books, 2016.

Keyser, Amber. *Tying the Knot: A World History of Marriage.* Minneapolis: Twenty-First Century Books, 2018.

Kops, Deborah. *Alice Paul and the Fight for Women's Rights.* Honesdale, PA: Calkin's Creek, 2017.

Wang, Tova Andrea. *The Politics of Voter Suppression: Defending and Expanding Americans' Right to Vote.* Ithaca, NY: Cornell University Press, 2012.

Wittenstein, Vicky Oransky. *Reproductive Rights: Who Decides?* Minneapolis: Twenty-First Century Books, 2016.

Websites

American Civil Liberties Union (ACLU)
https://www.aclu.org
Founded in 1920, the ACLU is devoted to defending the rights of freedoms of American citizens. Its website includes articles on voting rights, voter registration, and voting issues in the courts.

Black Girls Vote

> http://blackgirlsvote.com
> Founded in 2015, Black Girls Vote aims to inspire women of color to use the political process to improve lives for themselves and their families.

HeadCount

> https://www.headcount.org
> HeadCount is dedicated to helping Americans exercise their right to vote. The group focuses on registering young voters at concerts or other events.

League of Women Voters

> https://www.lwv.org/
> In 1920 Carrie Chapman Catt founded the League of Women Voters to ensure that women would be well informed when they went to the polls. Still in operation, the nonpartisan association hosts candidate debates, helps register new voters, and puts out voters' guides, explaining ballot measures and listing candidates' positions on key issues.

National Organization for Women (NOW)

> https://now.org
> Formed in 1966 by feminist activist Betty Friedan, NOW fights for women's rights and equality in employment, education, health care, and family life.

National Woman's Party

> https://www.nationalwomansparty.org
> Founded by Alice Paul in 1913, the National Woman's Party is still working for women's equality in politics and all aspects of American life.

Rock the Vote

> https://www.rockthevote.org
> Rock the Vote challenges young people to know their voting rights, register to vote, encourage others to vote, and use their votes to make positive change.

Susan B. Anthony Center

> http://www.rochester.edu/sba/suffrage-history
> Housed at the University of Rochester in New York, the Susan B. Anthony Center houses materials on the history of women's suffrage. The website offers biographies of suffragists, a timeline of the US suffrage movement, and other resources.

Voto Latino

> http://votolatino.org
> Cofounded by actor Rosario Dawson, Voto Latino began as an effort to register and educate Latino voters but has grown to advocate for Latinos in social justice, immigration and citizenship, and health care.

Films

Answering the Call: The American Struggle for the Right to Vote. DVD. San Diego: Riot House Pictures, 2016.
> This film tells the story of the voting rights struggle in Selma, Alabama, in 1965. It moves to the second decade of the twenty-first century, when many Americans' voting rights are still being suppressed.

Iron Jawed Angels. DVD. New York: HBO, 2004.
> Starring Hilary Swank as Alice Paul and Frances O'Connor as Lucy Burns, this historical drama presents a slightly fictionalized take on the US suffrage movement, from the 1913 suffrage parade in Washington, DC, through passage of the Nineteenth Amendment. The film focuses particularly on the picketing, arrests, imprisonment, and force-feedings of the silent sentinels.

One Woman, One Vote. DVD. Arlington, VA: Public Broadcasting Service, 2006.
> This documentary film explores the women's suffrage movement, from the 1848 Seneca Falls Convention to ratification of the Nineteenth Amendment.

Suffragette. DVD. Los Angeles: 20th Century Fox, 2015.
> This historical drama starring Carey Mulligan, Helena Bonham Carter, and Meryl Streep presents a somewhat fictionalized account of the woman suffrage movement in Britain, focusing especially on the efforts of working-class women.

INDEX

PHOTO ACKNOWLEDGMENTS

Image credits: Backgrounds: Douglas Sacha/Moment/Getty Images. Content: Library of Congress pp. 5 (LC-USZ62-70382), 9 (left) (LC-USZ61-1608), 9 (right) (LC-USZ61-1609), 15, 30 (LC-USZ62-119343), 52 (LC-USZ61-788), 56, 73; Bettmann Archive/Getty Images, p. 8; Walter Oleksy/Alamy Stock Photo, p. 20; Universal History Archive/Getty Images, p. 22; Bettmann Archive/Getty Images, p. 26; Library of Congress/Getty Images, p. 28; Fotosearch/Getty Images, p. 38; Fine Art Images/Heritage Images/Getty Images, p. 43; Fotosearch/Getty Images, p. 45; Alamy Stock Photo, p. 50; Everett Collection Inc/Alamy Stock Photo, pp. 58, 75; Jimmy Sime/Central Press/Hulton Archive/Getty Images, p. 63; Photo by Bain News Service/Library of Congress/Corbis/VCG/Getty Images, p. 65; Interim Archives/ Getty Images, p. 70; Corbis/Getty Images, p. 78; Hartsook/Library of Congress/ Corbis/VCG/Getty Images, p. 81; Bettmann Archive/Getty Images, p. 84; Charles Moore/Getty Images, p. 86; William Lovelace/Express/Getty Images, p. 87; Vicky Kasala/Digital Vision/Getty Images, p. 89; Joe Amon/The Denver Post/Getty Images, p. 91; Mario Tama/Getty Images, p. 96; Michael Kovac/Getty Images, p. 97; FREDERIC J. BROWN/AFP/Getty Images, p. 101.

Cover: Discan/DigitalVision Vectors/Getty Images; Eli_Oz/Shutterstock.com (fists); Annareichel/Shutterstock.com (bracelet).

ABOUT THE AUTHOR

Coral Celeste Frazer has a master's degree in sociology from Princeton University and a long-standing interest in issues of social justice. She writes nonfiction and fiction for teens and adults, as well as reading comprehension items for the Test of English as a Foreign Language. Her YA title *Economic Inequality: The American Dream under Siege* garnered star reviews from *Booklist* and *Kirkus Reviews*. She lives in Norwich, England, with her husband and son. To learn more about her, visit https://www.coralcelestefrazer.com.